DIALOGUES IN AMERICANISM

DIALOGUES
IN AMERICANISM

STEVE ALLEN
vs.
WILLIAM F. BUCKLEY JR.
November 17, 1963

ROBERT M. HUTCHINS
vs.
L. BRENT BOZELL
January 22, 1964

JAMES MacGREGOR BURNS
vs.
WILLMOORE KENDALL
February 23, 1964

 HENRY REGNERY CO.
CHICAGO 60610

PREFACE

This series of three debates was held at Pasadena, California on November 17, 1963, January 22, 1964, and February 23, 1964—each in the order in which it appears in this book. Held under the auspices of the Graduate Committee for Political Education Inc.—a non-profit corporation of graduate students from Harvard Law School, Wabash College, and California Institute of Technology—these debates were arranged in the hope that the confrontation of opposing points of view—the liberal and conservative points of view—would result in a more enlightened student community and general public in Southern California. It remained for Regnery editor Jameson G. Campaigne, Jr. to propose that we put the debates in book form for the benefit, and delight, of others.

The debates would not have been the success they were without the unflagging assistance of a number of individuals and organizations in Southern California. Our moderator for the series, Mr. Homer Odom, vice-president and general manager of X-TRA News in Los Angeles, did a superb job of assuring an entertaining and orderly program, and was most kind in seeing that we had adequate radio publicity. Mr. Richard Mainland, our secretary, and Mr. John Harmer, who did excellent public relations work, were absolutely invaluable in their assistance. The San Fernando Valley Business and Professional Men's Association lent needed help, as did the Young Republicans and Young Democrats and other organizations in Los Angeles.

The debates appear here as they were given, except for minor editing to assure consistency and to remove those linguistic devices appropriate to listening, but not to reading. Also, the question periods have been deleted. The order of debate in each case was determined by a flip of the coin.

The inclusion of the debate on John F. Kennedy's foreign policy was decided upon because, as both participants agreed, the issues are very much the same in 1964 as they were in 1963, and the debate was largely on the issues.

Michael Gazzaniga, *President*

THE GRADUATE COMMITTEE FOR POLITICAL EDUCATION

June 1, 1964

CONTENTS

Steve Allen

vs.

William F. Buckley Jr.

The Presidency

"Resolved: The foreign policy of
John F. Kennedy has been successful."

William F. Buckley Jr.

Opening Statement:

 S TEVE ALLEN told me last spring when we
met to consider this invitation that he had never before
in his entire life debated with anyone. That was of course
a joke; probably the only poor one he has ever made.
The remark, needless to say, was intended sincerely. The
worst thing about Steve Allen is that he sincerely believes
what he says. He meant to make a gesture of respect for
my allegedly superior experience. But consider whence
the compliment came: from a master verbalist, a born
showman, a fabulous extemporizer who, almost every
night, dating back to when I was a schoolboy being trained
to make the world safe for democracy, has faced vast
audiences, making them laugh or cry, feel happy or feel
sad, by the use of his great art. It is I who am destined
to play the fool for my cause, who have stepped in where
angels fear to tread.

In remarking his innocence of the science of debate he
meant, I suppose, to disarm me. Heaven only knows how
many weapons this great showman has neatly hidden in
that disarmingly unruffled suit (which I learned from a
recent advertisement in *Esquire* is "all wool"), how many

rabbits, pumpkins, balloons, lizards, dolls, saws, incenses, stink bombs are neatly tucked away there. One by one he will bring them out and hurl them against the impregnable virtue of my position.

I say impregnable because in the end I doubt that the magician lives who can make the case for the foreign policy of John F. Kennedy before an American audience. It takes a different audience to appreciate that case, from a different vantage point. Like a Russian audience.

Now, now, now, let me first of all make plain that I do not consider that Mr. Steve Allen is pro-Communist. Let me go further and say that I consider that any man who suspects him of being pro-Communist is evil or witless. Let me concede (for I know that the subject weighs heavily on Mr. Allen) that he has been treated outrageously by individual members of the so-called right. Let me concede that there are members of what goes by the name of "the right wing" who cherish a great ignorance of the realities. And let me say that some of these men and women, in pursuit of their fantasies, do damage to persons who are subjectively innocent of the offenses they are charged with. Such persons—some of them malicious, some of them mis-informed—exist on the right; but so do they exist on the left.

It was a half century ago that Chesterton complained of the allure that so-called "progressive" movements have for (as he put it) "every fruit juice drinker, nudist, sandal wearer, sex maniac, Quaker, pacifist, and feminist in England." He could have retained the list intact to describe many of the current admirers of Mr. Allen's position. There is, as I say, a lot of loose talk going on and California, is no doubt the world's principal exporter of it. I remember Mr. Stanley Mosk, California's Attorney General, saying a couple of years ago that the John

Birch Society was a collection of "little old ladies in tennis shoes." And now Mr. Mosk has informed a convention of California Democrats that the Republican party is in danger of being taken over by the John Birch Society—raising the question whether he got hit on the head by a tennis shoe or whether he is just scared of little old ladies. But we are not here tonight to talk about eccentrics, we are here to talk about the foreign policy of Mr. Kennedy, and never mind why it appeals to eccentrics. We wish to know, what is worse still, why it appeals to non-eccentrics.

In assessing the foreign policy of *any* administration, it is always possible to dwell on a single success or on a single failure and go on to construct an apology or an indictment on the basis of it. Much of what passes for objective evaluation is based on selectivity of this kind. In meditating on liberalism, its foreign policy and the shambles thereof, I am reminded of the man who, having heard a direful sermon on the subject of the Ten Commandments, walked out of the Church alongside his wife, with head bowed, looking neither to right nor to left. Suddenly, approaching his car, his eyes lit up. He turned to his wife jubilantly: "I just remembered—I've never made any graven images!" So a defender of Mr. Kennedy might say that after all, he has not yet turned Washington over to the Communists—at least not *all* of Washington. (Having read last week about the twentieth or so Communist spy caught within the past nine months, I recall morosely Bob Hope's statement on returning this summer from abroad, that "in England there is the best secret service in the world. The trouble is the Russians own it.")

Under the circumstances, in an attempt to avoid polemical selectivity, I shall permit an official spokesman for liberalism no less authoritative than Mr. Lyndon Johnson to select three areas for discussion. "During the campaign of 1964," Mr. Johnson said last October, "this administration will go to the people and defend its foreign policy on the basis of its record in Berlin, Laos, and Cuba."

1–Whence the triumph of Berlin? Because West Berliners are still free? But it does not prove success merely to prove that all is not yet lost. West Berliners are still relatively free, true; but Berlin is a sundered city because President Kennedy, who alone could have prevented it, permitted its division. He had no idea, he told the press early in 1962, that the Soviet Union had been preparing during the preceding July to build a wall through the city. I believe him. (Although as I remarked at the time, it is extraordinary that such large reserves of standby brick and mortar could have escaped the attention even of our CIA.) Even so, the deed was done. Subsequently, the West has stood firm in denying the balance of the city to Mr. Khrushchev, whose appetite for it has sharpened precisely because of the ease with which he had succeeded in planting down the wall.

But whose fortitude is today responsible for the maintenance of a free West Berlin? It is widely known that Mr. Kennedy and his aides sought to discuss with the Russians (under the pressure of the Soviet ultimatum) alternatives to the present arrangements more satisfactory to them. But it is known that Charles de Gaulle flatly refused, for so long as Berlin was being illegally threatened, to participate in any discussion whatsoever over its future. It is generally accepted, in other words, that it was the granitic de Gaulle who provided the stamina on which West Berlin survives. And indeed it is conjectured—and one has no alternative to conjecture when discussing an administration which has developed so effectively the science of

news management—that one of the reasons why Mr.
de Gaulle has shown an increasing reluctance to rely on
American foreign policy, is because American foreign
policy is not reliable. One is never quite sure whether, at a
critical moment in Western affairs, the chiefs-of-staff will
make the operative decisions or Mr. Norman Cousins will.
Others have leaned on American foreign policy over the
years—Poles, Czechs, Chinese and Tibetans; Cubans and
Laotians; and Vietnamese. The crowning pity is that
Americans have to rely on American foreign policy.

2–The claim that Mr. Johnson can point to *Cuba* as a
victory for his foreign policy is a venture in utter audacity.
It is as though Mr. Hoover had run for re-election in 1932
on the basis of the raging national prosperity. I have written a great deal about the Cuban disaster and tried to
analyze it at some length; and I have spent my rhetoric on
the subject. I do not have the stomach to restate the case,
any more than some of you have the stomach to hear it.
I can only reassert, in the simplest terms, my conviction
that our failure to move decisively against Castro continues as the most conspicuous symptom of our de-
generacy.

What will bring this administration to save Cuba?
Nothing, presumably; unless Castro finds a few Buddhists
to persecute. It appears to be safe to say that we *have* no
policy as regards Cuba. Our policy towards Cuba is to
behave towards it peevishly. We address her, from within
our fastness, with the petulance of the prudent man who
has been bested in an encounter, dares not risk another,
but for vanity's sake needs to keep his tongue stuck out
at his adversary. Mr. Kennedy's solemn retaliation against
Cuba's importation of the thermonuclear intermediate

range missiles was to forbid American tourists to visit
Cuba. It was the Cuban admittance of the missiles that
was apparently the unfriendly act—not the Russian-
manufactured transportation and installation of same, we
are to gather from the workings of Mr. Kennedy's
foreign policy. After all, we *do* allow American tourists
to go to the Soviet Union (in fact, encourage them to go
there); and we do allow our wheat to go to the Soviet
Union; but not to Cuba—no sir, no señor, not Mr. Kennedy.

And then, to drive home the dead seriousness of our
Cuba policy, Mr. Kennedy devoted a whole speech to the
subject of the forthcoming liberation of Cuba before sur-
vivors of the Bay of Pigs invasion assembled at the Orange
Bowl in Miami, one paragraph of which Mrs. Kennedy
spoke in Spanish. Why he was not torn limb from limb by
that company of soldiers betrayed, I'll never know. I finally
understand the meaning of the mañana attitude.

Our policy as regards Cuba will, then, presumably bear
fruit (like our so-called policy toward Hungary) on the day
when we will have resumed diplomatic relations; as we
have for all intents and purposes done under Mr. Kennedy
with Hungary. Do not ask what American foreign policy
has accomplished in Hungary, or what it is accomplishing
in Cuba; to do so would be to disconcert non-debaters.
In fact, Hungary yielded nothing. Not freedom for the
students of Budapest. Not even freedom for the mortal
remains of Imre Nagy, whose bones the government refuses to return to his family. When Mr. Kennedy's present
policy toward Cuba reaches its radiant fruition, i.e. when
we agree to give Cuba not only our drugs but *also* our
tourists and our wheat, Cuba will still be free to conspire
against us, against our people, and against our truths
everywhere in the hemisphere by the continued use of

guile, subversion, treachery, blasphemy, torture. Ask not what Cuba can do for us, ask what we can do for Cuba.

3–In Laos we triumphed under Mr. Kennedy by refusing to give aid to the anti-Communist forces who were resisting a coalition government with the neutralists and the pro-Communists.

Here is the background of *that* triumph! In Moscow, Mr. Khrushchev told Mr. Harriman that if he would bring pressure to bear on President Kennedy to consent to the coalition government, he, Khrushchev, would promise to see to it that the Communist and pro-Communist members of the coalition behave; would see to it, presumably, that they cease to be Communists, since nothing short of that would cause them to behave. Intoxicated by that news, Mr. Harriman rushed back to Washington and in a matter of weeks the triumph was consummated.

So taken was the New Frontier by this new mode in diplomacy that in due course Mr. Harriman was bounced back to Moscow, where he got a still further promise from the Soviet government to behave in respect to nuclear testing, whence the derivative triumph of the Treaty of Moscow, the test-ban treaty. Just eight years ago, surveying the Spirit of Geneva proclaimed by President Eisenhower, Mr. Harriman had publicly proclaimed, "Unhappily, at the conference of the Summit, President Eisenhower was quoted as crediting the Russians with no less a desire for peace than that of the West. As a consequence, there occurred a psychological disarmament throughout the free world. It is a tragedy," he concluded, "that the President didn't do something *else*. He did mention, but he did not keep insisting, that Stalin should carry out his wartime agreements, to permit free elections in Poland and Eastern Europe."

But when psychological disarmament is administered by Mr. Harriman himself, in behalf of the Democratic Party, it is something else, is it not? It is a triumph. Ask Lyndon Johnson. Ask Steve Allen. Ask a cuckoo clock.

We are living, ladies and gentlemen, in an age when direct communication becomes increasingly difficult. We need to rely increasingly, those of us in any case who care, on a kind of Aesopian prose which at the ordinary level says one thing, but if you listen very very hard, and if you are truly disposed to hear, is saying something very different. We all know that a political party must defend its record, for such are the iron requirements of partisan politics. But the present administration seeks to defend its record by paying the conventional obeisances to traditional policy, at the same time suggesting, sometimes explicitly, more often subliminally, the necessity for "new approaches;" the common factor of which is appeasement.

The policy suggested by George Kennan when he wrote in *Foreign Affairs* on the necessity for containment we practiced intermittently as for instance at Iran and South Korea under Mr. Truman; and under Mr. Eisenhower at Lebanon and Quemoy. But even under the rubric of Kennan's policy Czechoslovakia fell; as did China; as did Tibet and Cuba; as, for all intents and purposes, did Indonesia and British Guiana. But the policy of containment remained, nevertheless, as the official paradigm: the policy that under no circumstances whatever will the Soviet Union be permitted to advance its imperialism over any area not already subjugated in 1947.

The policy was never inherently sound for the reason that it was dogmatically *defensive*, and failed to reckon with the advantages that go to the side that monopolizes the initiative. The policy of containment is based on repressing the enemy's salients rather than striking our own. Trotsky told his generals, when on one occasion they asked him how most profitably to pursue the war against the capitalist world, that the Soviet high command must constantly gyrate a finger around the perimeter of the enemy world. "And where it probes a weakness, *there*," said Trotsky, "is our salient."

And so the Communists over the years have been operating. They have not looked alone for military weaknesses in contiguous geographical areas, though they probed these too; they looked for weaknesses of *every* kind: weaknesses in our economy; weaknesses in our race relations; weakness in our system of alliances; weakness in our internal security; weakness in our military technology; weakness, above all, in our soul. And it is these weaknesses, above all others, that they have feasted upon; for at the moments of truth in great battlefronts merely suggested by the place-names Warsaw, Budapest, Berlin, Peking, it was not a lack of Western power that proved decisive, but a lack of Western will. Our policy postulated no salients of our own, even on ascertaining gaping weaknesses in the enemy:

When she is militarily weak as after the last war, we stand by and let her acquire nuclear weapons. When she is guilty of a fresh act of aggression as at Berlin, we close ranks against Tshombe in Katanga and censure South Africa. When she staggers from a moral wound as after Budapest, we initiate cultural exchanges. When she desires a temporary cessation of certain types of nuclear testing, we go to Moscow and sign the dotted line. When her agricultural program collapses, we send her wheat.

We permit ourselves only counter-salient expressions of life: They fight us in Korea, we fight back in Korea. They fight us in Viet Nam, we fight them in Viet Nam. They threaten Lebanon, we land troops in Lebanon. They bomb Quemoy, we fortify Quemoy. But now, even that policy of containment seems to be requiring an effort beyond the will of the American government to generate. In the past three years, we tried, because of the forward inertia still left in the old idea, to generate the counter-salient in Cuba; but we could not arouse ourself off the beach. In Laos, instead of countering the offensive decisively, we retreated behind the skirts of neutralism. In Berlin, we did not tear down the wall, but learned instead to live under its humiliating shadow. Again in Cuba, we retreated on our demand to inspect the Russian missile bases.

But meanwhile, the *rhetoric* of defiance, even of liberation, continues as a basso sostenuto throughout our strategic variations. I could not myself, in my most abandoned moments of hope, compose a speech more inspiring to direct action against Castro than Mr. Kennedy's, delivered to the ransomed Cuban prisoners in Miami about three weeks before he cracked down on every Cuban who was subsequently engaged in trying to do something about the liberation of his homeland, i.e. every Cuban who at Miami took Mr. Kennedy at his word. Who would guess that the speech delivered at American University in Washington last June, calling for an end even to *philosophical* differences with the Soviet Union, and that given in August in Berlin calling for victory over the Soviet Union at any cost, had been delivered by the same man?

There is at work against us an assault on the meaning of words, those instruments of civilization by which we communicate with one another and correspond with our governors. Would that we could have a treaty suspending the abuse of rhetoric! The worst enemy of America is the debauchery of language, the loss of whose meaning would deprive us even of the power to express our fear of the abomination of desolation.

"I have sometimes thought," Albert J. Nock wrote in his last years, "that it would be interesting to write an essay on the subject of 'How One Can Tell One Is Living in a Dark Age.' " I have never doubted that George Orwell, writing 10 years later, gave Nock the answer when he wrote his incandescent novel about the society whose tablets proclaim that War is Peace, Freedom is Slavery, Ignorance is Strength. The trouble with our foreign policy is less its intrinsic defects than that men of intelligence and good will actually rise to defend it.

Steve Allen

Opening Statement:

GOOD EVENING conservatives, liberals, and
little old ladies in tennis shoes or not. It was apparent to
Mr. Buckley and myself as we stood backstage listening to
the opening remarks, that this audience tonight was a very
special one and that it was absolutely determined to de-
rive enormous emotional satisfaction from whatever might
occur on the stage here. I would by no means seek to deny
any audience emotional satisfaction; I would simply suggest that we make the attempt to distinguish emotional
satisfaction from wisdom, from the accumulation of necessary information. Perhaps I should next point out that I
am not officially or unofficially representing the President.
I represent only myself. I shall consider my time not wasted
this evening (and I direct this remark to my fellow citizens in the conservative camp who are present) if even a
few of my ideas succeed in penetrating the screen of your
prejudices—the screen of your prejudices and your long-
denied hunger for political representation. (Human nature
being what it is, I don't object at all to a few cat-calls and
boos when I use the word prejudices, but I would hope
that you would at least grant that we all *have* prejudices.)

Mr. Buckley has just finished demonstrating his skill at polemics. Many of you, especially those in his own camp, are of course familiar with him. But some here are familiar with him only slightly perhaps, or in a general way, so I will take just a moment to tell you something about Mr. Buckley (since doing so may help you put what he tells us this evening in better perspective. And also since he has established, a few minutes ago, precedent for remarks of this kind by references to my tailoring and so forth).

Mr. Buckley, as you have seen, is not only a gifted speaker and writer, but he is also a very courageous man. Indeed he has been courageous enough to do battle in print with the late Pope John XXIII concerning matters on which the Pope was expert, and he was not. And that not once, but repeatedly (going so far on one occasion as to refer to the historically important papal encyclical *Mater et Magistra* as "a venture in triviality"). Now Mr. Buckley, as you have seen, is a wonderfully entertaining man; and we might be tempted to interpret such a statement as indicating nothing more than a "Groucho Marxish" desire to shock. But such is not the case. Mr. Buckley *does* indeed feel that, in the context of the fearful struggle between Western man and the forces of Communism, Pope John's admonitions concerning social justice *were* truly trivial. All of which has lead me to compose two limerick paragraphs describing my distinguished opponent:

> There is a young man named Bill Buck-i-ly
> Who debates all the liberals quite pluckily
> When all's said and done,
> It must be just in fun,
> For few are persuaded—quite luckily.

He selects foes with great impartiality
Sans regards for race, creed, or nationality,
But he makes some mistakes,
And the worst of his breaks
Was that "venture in—uh—triviality."

Mr. Buckley and I have fortunately nothing worth dueling about; we are not enemies, but friends. And had I any interest in somehow defeating him, as distinguished from merely rubbing our conflicting ideas together in the hope that the sparks might provide some intellectual light, I would certainly never have selected the weapon of formal debate (at which Mr. Buckley is apparently undisputed champion, not only because of his erudition, but because of his uncanny gift for sarcasm, for the creation of political poetry, and a dramatic delivery reminiscent of Lionel Barrymore's). And now to work!

In any debate on foreign policy today, between any conservative and any liberal, the conservative of course has one advantage; and that is that he has nothing practical to defend. Today's conservative has not put a team on the ballfield, whereas the liberals have; and therefore the conservative can point to the mistakes that the liberal team has made. What the liberals *can* do to counter is to say, "Well we see no reason to believe that had your team played the game, it would have played it any better. And there are those who believe it would have played it a good deal worse." But what's important to understand is that there is no way whatsoever to settle that issue. The only method by which the opposing arguments could be logically tested would be to turn back the clock of history and simply live again through the events of the last twenty-five or fifty years, depending on how far back one might want to go, to get a running head start on the difficult problems looming up. That, of course, is fantasy. As regards reality, the issue simply cannot be settled.

I ask you to consider next the very great improbability that any one program, be it conservative, liberal, or what-have-you, is a golden key which would magically open all doors and solve all difficult problems. Now Americans are a practical people—very few of us are philosophers, few of us are artists, few of us are scholars; but many of us are tinkerers and bookkeepers and businessmen. We tend, therefore, to desire solutions that are simple, sensible, and brass tacks. Our popular magazines are full of articles which favor the perpetuation of such attitudes: how to play the piano in ten easy lessons, five rules for personal happiness, seven ways to a successful marriage, and so forth. Quite aside from the fact that such solutions usually do not teach us to play the piano, improve our marriages and our personal lives, there is no question but that the simplistic approach to such a matter as foreign policy brings about little but frustration. The world is so incredibly complex today that it is perhaps a blessing for the average man that he is unable to appreciate the dimensions of its complexity. Perhaps if he really understood how difficult our problems are, he would not be able to sleep at night.

For example, we are currently doing business with 112 other nations, and about 40 of them will be changing governments during the coming year—and not all peaceably. The tides of history are sweeping high and fast. We live, indeed, in a time of great danger, but also great challenge. It is no time to listen to voices of pessimism or defeat or empty bluster. Influential right-wing spokesmen, whom I am happy to say Mr. Buckley has personally disallowed, have apparently induced some Americans to believe that by 1972 the Communists plan to take over the United States. Is comment really necessary? Now a conservative gentleman wrote to me some time ago that the foreign policy of the U.S. is or should be "the defeat of Communism." But this is like saying that the Christian religion *is* the salvation of souls. No, the Christian faith is a *means* toward the salvation of souls. The two things, in other words, are distinct, though related.

As regards the ultimate defeat of the forces of Communism, that is the most appealing idea in the world, however interpreted. The foreign policy of the United States *may* or *may not* bring such an ideal to realization, but what is important for us to appreciate is that the two are distinct.

It will be helpful, in attempting to understand what a nation's foreign policy is, if you think of the word "policy" not as suggesting a single sentence stating a lofty aim, but rather in the sense in which it is used in the phrase "insurance policy." An insurance policy, as we know (sometimes to our chagrin!), is quite a lengthy document; and yet it covers particulars that, compared to the conduct of the nation's foreign relations, are simplicity itself. I say this because you are daily being lead to believe that Communist advances are explained either chiefly or *solely* because of what American foreign policy is, for better or for worse. And I tell you this is nonsense.

Now I am sure you would agree that the average United States *senator* knows a great deal more about foreign policy than does the average *citizen*; and I imagine that most of you would be as willing to grant that in the Senate, the average member of the committee on Foreign Relations knows *somewhat* more about foreign policy than does the average senator *not* a member of that committee. I solicit your consent on these generalities by way of drawing attention to the following specifics:

In 1958, the Committee on Foreign Relations of the Senate, having realized that its members were experiencing difficulty in getting questions of foreign policy into sharp focus, established a special subcommittee consisting of Senators Green, Fulbright, Wiley, and Hickenlooper, and instructed it to explore the feasibility of an extensive study of our nation's foreign policy. Subsequently the subcommittee reported it was possible to undertake such a study, which the subcommittee believed would lead to a better national understanding of international problems. At this point the members of the subcommittee turned to various private research organizations by way of assuring that our nation's best minds would concentrate their creative attentions to the problems at hand. (The intellectuals employed by these distinguished research organizations are those terrible "eggheads"—commonly referred to so derisively in the conservative press.)

On January 5, 1959, it was announced that the following studies were being undertaken:

1–the nature of foreign policy and the role of the United States in the world; 2–the operational aspects of U.S. foreign policy; 3–the principal ideological conflicts and their present and potential impact on foreign policy; 4–world-wide and domestic economic problems and their impact on foreign policy; 5–foreign policy implications for the United States of economic and social conditions in lesser-developed and uncommitted countries; 6–possible developments in military technology, their influence on strategic doctrine, and the impact of such developments on U.S. foreign policy; 7–possible non-military, scientific developments and their potential impact on foreign policy; 8–formulation and administration of U.S. foreign policy; 9–U.S. foreign policy in Western Europe; 10–U.S. foreign policy in the U.S.S.R. and Eastern Europe; 11–U.S. foreign policy in the Near East; 12–U.S. foreign policy in Southeast Asia; 13–U.S. foreign policy in Africa.

Now I suggest that if the members of the United States

Senate who are most conversant with foreign policy problems felt that they absolutely required this sort of backing in helping them to understand the difficult area which is *their professional specialty*, it would be presumptuous for those of us who are less well-informed to assume that all there is to this business of foreign policy is asserting that we are determined to "defeat the Communists" and then just rolling up our sleeves and going out and doing it.

Now if there is anything that today's conservatives find annoying, it is the criticism that Senator Goldwater is forever suggesting simplistic solutions for complex problems; but the conservative camp had better get ready to feel good and annoyed for many months to come, because the Senator deserves precisely this sort of criticism. Indeed, the only way he can put a stop to it is to throw overboard his past recommendations and replace them with some that have a lesser burden of belligerence and a greater part of wisdom and originality.

But I am here tonight to make a more important point, and it is that to a certain extent we are almost *all* guilty of Senator Goldwater's sin. The United States has been a long time developing its present sense of international maturity and responsibility. Traditionally we were suspicious and uneasy, as some of us still are, about what we call "foreign entanglements." We had the Atlantic and Pacific to protect us and weak neighbors to the north and south, so we felt secure in our isolation. Isolationism, of course, is not solely indigenous to the American continent. In fact, the very word is a euphemism for one that is more familiar: selfishness. We are then ignorant and selfish, not because we are Americans, but because we are human. It was an Englishman, Neville Chamberlain, speaking on December 26, 1938, who said the British people ought not to be expected to involve themselves in the approaching war because of "a quarrel in a far away country between people of whom we know nothing." That far away country, as you know, was Czechoslovakia.

I wonder if man has now learned the lesson that *there are no longer any far away countries*. Morally, there never were. Morally, we were always supposed to know that we are our brothers' keepers. Morally, those of us who preach the Fatherhood of God should always have known that the brotherhood of man follows logically. But now, what irony! Now, for the most selfish of reasons, we can no longer afford to be selfish

One of our foreign policy triumphs was the Marshall plan. The Marshall Plan restored the economic strength of Western Europe after World War II, and this, my friends, was *real* anti-Communism. The kind that not only helped the West, but *hurt actual Communists*. But it was resisted by congressional isolationists, and to this very day Senator Goldwater says that "the foreign aid program has had dire consequences. The foreign aid program is unconstitutional, and is not only ill-considered, but ill-conceived. It has not made the free world stronger," the Senator continued, "it has made America weaker."

After isolationism, I would list *ignorance* as an important cause contributing to our present dilemma. We have belatedly begun to do our international homework but, if I had time this evening, I could tell you some hair-raising stories of American ignorance, in high places and low, concerning the rest of the world and its peoples. Just for a moment, test your own geographical knowledge (and none of us, of course, could score a hundred points on this kind of a test): Could you point to Indonesia on the map? Are you aware that it has a population of 100 million people, the fifth largest in the world? Are you aware that potentially it is the fourth richest nation in the world? If you are . . . good for you.

Next on our list of complicating factors, I would include

the delusion of omnipotence. This is a very important point: even if we made all the right decisons, the fact remains that we do not run the world. Not only can we not dictate to our enemies or to the neutrals, we cannot even dictate to our allies. The Communist powers *are* loosely united, at least, in working toward their large goal. The free world, on the other hand, is merely a group of rival, individualistic states that even today compete for advantage or prestige just as they did during the long centuries of European history. Now let those who are surprised that the West cannot completely unite to fight Communism remember that even when the nations of Europe were all securely under the banner of Christendom, or indeed even when they all professed allegiance to the one Catholic Church, they were still regularly at each other's throats. This is political reality, and we forget it at our peril.

And now a word in defense of our critics on the right. It is sometimes said that conservatives don't really believe the scare talk they broadcast, to the effect that the Communists are steadily winning the cold war while we are constantly retreating, failing and so forth. It is claimed that critics of the administration deliberately distort reality to this extent because they know that if they can alarm enough voters, a change in administrations might take place. But I believe that the critics on the right are completely sincere in their criticism. Sincere, and frequently as wrong as Hell. The way they tell it, the Communists are winning the game all the way, and nothing short of putting in a new coach could save the day. Nonsense. *Certainly* there have been Communist victories, and they are enough to cause us the gravest concern. But there have been hopeful developments too, and we must look at the total picture, not just that part of it that satisfies either our emotional predispositions or our political ambitions. Consider the following:

1–in Berlin, though the wall is still up (I will be talking later about the suggestion that we break it down), the Russians now know that we cannot be either bluffed or forced out of the city. And the wall, despite its ugliness, is a tremendous propaganda plus for our side. The Communists are no more proud of it than they were of putting down the Hungarian uprising. 2–in the Congo, we stuck with the United Nations, contrary to Senator Goldwater's advice. Order has been restored and Russian desires frustrated. 3–in the Middle East, the Communists have suffered major setbacks during the past year, particularly in Iraq. In Egypt, though the Russians have poured in millions of dollars in aid, they have not reaped a corresponding political influence.* 4–since the attack on India by Red China, relations between India and the United States are considerably improved. Nehru learned his lesson the hard way, and the result is a gain for our side. 5–in Algeria, which conservatives had told us was lost to the Communists, a government that is socialist, but neutral, has emerged. And our timely foreign aid has helped us win a significant degree of Algerian friendship. 6–in Cuba, Soviet missiles have been withdrawn and so have thousands of Soviet personnel, if not enough. Though Castro is still in power, it costs the Soviet Union a million dollars a day to keep him propped up. He is no longer as popular throughout Latin America as he was a year or two ago, and there are signs that another invasion by Cubans and sympathetic forces may be in the planning stage. 7–since Hiroshima, the world's spiritual shepherds, philosophers, scientists, and political leaders have pointed out the dangers of approaching nuclear war. Pope Pius XII, for example, called the nuclear arms race "homicidal, suicidal madness." Now,

* This statement was true in late 1963 but Khrushchev's recent visit to Egypt makes it necessary to review the situation in that nation— S. A., June, 1964.

at last, a test-ban treaty has been signed. It is, as President
Kennedy has said, only the small first step on a thousand
mile journey to peace; and we don't even know if another
step ever will be taken. But the overwhelming majority of
the world's peoples rejoice that it has been taken. 8–Mr.
Buckley has referred to the Truman Doctrine containment
policy. I say that though it deals only with the matter of
military encroachment, it has on the whole accomplished
its objective: to convince the Soviets that they would not
be permitted to conquer additional territory. We made this
clear in Greece and Turkey, and we showed our determination concerning Korea, Formosa, and the offshore
islands.

9–NATO exists and represents a Western success. In
the early post-war years, the Communist parties of Western Europe were very strong and very threatening. Today,
they are no more dangerous than they were then.

[*Following a rash of cat-calls and boos from the audience, Mr. Allen made this statement—Ed.*]:

*I'm going to interrupt my formal remarks to give you
a suggestion. I accepted this debate because, as I pointed
out, Bill and I are friends of quite a long time standing,
and because I have attempted on a number of occasions
to make public the distinction between the respectable conservatives in this country, a number of whom besides Bill
are among my personal friends, and the irresponsibles. I
think responsible conservative voices are utterly necessary
in the present difficult moment, and Mr. Buckley's magazine has done a great deal to distinguish between the intelligent conservatives, and the people (to use Mr. Nixon's
phrase) who are described as "the nuts and the kooks."
Now any time you get several thousand people in one
room, it's inevitable, no matter what they are—they can
all be liberals, all be anything—you will inevitably have a*

few nuts and kooks. But I ask the nuts and kooks here this evening to shut up, not because it is the easiest way in the world to deal with them (since I am by twenty years of professional training equipped to handle hecklers), but because it represents a foolish digression from our central purposes. These debates, the series of debates, are being staged by an organization that I respect and admire, a responsible conservative organization. And their loud-mouth representatives here are doing them no credit. So for your own sake, if you want these next two debates to occur, please conduct yourselves like ladies and gentlemen— those of you who are not. 10–the transition out of the long period of colonialism, an era which, never let us forget, involved actual slavery, has been made rather more peaceably than the historians may have anticipated. The angry debate is substantially over, and the new nations now know that our face is not set against them. I shudder to think how the United States would have dealt with the anti-colonialist upsurge had a conservative administration been in power.

Now these observations obviously do not give the whole picture, but they are sufficient to establish my point. So, it may be arguable as to how good a senator Mr. Goldwater has been; but it is undeniable that he is a successful businessman. When I lived in Phoenix, Arizona in the early forties, he was even then successfully running the department store his father had left him. He therefore must know a great deal about bookkeeping; but what sort of foreign policy bookkeeping is it to list *only debts and losses* and pay no attention whatsoever to profits? It may eventually appear this evening that I am debating Senator Goldwater, rather than Mr. Buckley. I plead guilty to that charge; Bill Buckley is a more formidable opponent than the Senator. Bill is an intellectual and a skillful debater. Mr. Goldwater, who is a fine man in many respects, is neither. Now let us take up his foreign policy views.

It is the Senator who is the leader of the present conservative movement, and one is certainly entitled to take up the question as to what might result in the event he became our President. *National Review* magazine once editorialized as follows: "What Mr. Kennedy has discovered during his first 100 days is that being President and facing up to the Communists is far more difficult than subjugating the Democratic Party or impressing the American people." This, of course, is what every modern President has learned and will learn. So Mr. Goldwater would discover first that he faces the same dilemmas faced by Messrs. Truman, Eisenhower, and Kennedy. He would find that it is the easiest thing in the world to criticize from outside the palace gates, but that when one is on the inside, problems that may have appeared simple loom in sharp focus and terrifying complexity.

Because the Senator is a completely honest man, I therefore conclude that being President of the United States would be an enormously frustrating and humiliating experience for him, and I'll explain that. Consider the following evidence: he has now for several years, as James Reston of *The New York Times* has observed, entertained the illogical belief that our nation can on the one hand significantly decrease the power of the Federal government and greatly reduce the budget, while on the other it can be harder on the Communists all over the world. The Senator has been arguing that we should do more with our military power to oppose the expansion of Communist influence. He has recommended blockading Cuba indefinitely, which naturally would mean stopping Russian and perhaps other ships going into Havana. But he has not made clear what he would recommend if the Russians appeared determined to run the blockade, or what he would do if, in retaliation, they began to stop our ships carrying arms to Turkey or some other nation.

Now it's of enormous importance in this connection that the editors of *National Review* have long been calling for, not merely air cover for invasions of Cuba by natives of that island, but outright war and invasion by the United States. The reason this is important is that it is these gentlemen and their colleagues who tell Mr. Goldwater much of what he thinks, since he is himself neither a political philosopher nor a man accustomed to wielding power. There is yet additional inconsistency in his attitude toward the nuclear weapons dilemma: he asserts he does not want to see the uncontrolled spread of nuclear weapons, but on the other hand, he is against the administration's disarmament, arms control, and nuclear testing recommendations.

Next item: he approves of any actions that would tend to introduce wedges into the Communist bloc, any ventures that would tend to pit one Communist nation against the other—as for example, Russia against China. But on the other hand, he has said "we should withdraw diplomatic recognition from all Communist governments, including that of the Soviet Union." And these are not merely isolated instances. The Senator is opposed to Communist expansion into the newly emerging nations, but he voted *against* the Mutual Security Act in 1960 and is, as you have seen, hostile to almost all forms of foreign aid. It's no wonder then that the Senator's overall political program has been termed by Mr. Reston "a fantastic catalogue of contradictions."

Senator Goldwater is forever calling for, to use his own words, "total victory over Communism." But he has not made clear precisely what he *means* by "total victory," nor how he would achieve it if he did know exactly what it meant. The idea, however defined, is, as I say, unassailable. Certainly no American in his right mind would say he is opposed to total victory over Communism. But concentration on victory in these terms can mislead us into supposing that the day such victory was achieved would usher in a new millenium of prosperity and happiness. Unfortunately, if Communism were to disappear from the face of the earth this evening, tomorrow would still bring us an intricate array of problems. After all, the last two world wars ended in total victory, but they did not bring world-wide peace, prosperity, or social justice. Now does the Senator contemplate achieving his total victory by a nuclear attack on the Soviet Union? If the answer is yes (and I don't believe for a moment that it is), then I say whosoever does recommend such a course of action is a madman. If the answer is no, then I am sure we would all appreciate it if the Senator would say as much aloud, as soon as possible. Does the Senator contemplate achieving total victory over Communism by conventional war? I rather doubt this, too; but here again I wish he would answer yes or no soon to the simple proposition.

There are millions who look forward with happy anticipation to the day when he might be our Commander in Chief. And all of us have a right to know if on the day he is sworn into office, he plans to involve this nation in war, nuclear or conventional, with the Communist third of the world. If the Senator has no such intentions, which would seem to be the case, then we return to the question, What on earth does he mean by the phrase "total victory over Communism"? Now if I may offer the Senator a helpful suggestion, I would recommend that he consider that the word "victory" has more than one meaning, and that there is one interpretation of it which is in accord with the dictates of our national security, common sense, and morality. I refer to the two relevant definitions as the prize-fighting, and the horse-racing definitions. Victory can be achieved in a horse race and it can be achieved in the boxing ring. If the Senator believes it is possible, given the present military realities, to defeat the forces of Communism the way one prize fighter defeats another, by slugging him to the floor, then he has a great deal of explaining to do. But if he simply means that in the race between two rival ideologies we will win that race by finishing well ahead of the Communists, then he is being rational. (Unfortunately, he is not being very original since such victory is exactly what our present leadership is already striving to accomplish.)

Now conservatives assert that we must adopt an *offensive* strategy that is, as Mr. Bozell has written, "every bit as serious about liberating Communist territory as the Communists are about enslaving ours." Well, *where is* this offensive strategy? What are its particulars? It's occurred to me that one reason right-wing alternatives so often deal with wishful generalities rather than specifics is that on the rare occasions when practical suggestions are vouchsafed, they are so often seen as hollow bombast. Mr. Buckley has already told us (and *National Review* has been specific on this point) about the Berlin Wall. The solution: *break down the wall!* All right, let's think about that. This, of course, would be accomplished by an invasion of the Soviet sector of Berlin, since the wall is on that side of the boundary, you understand. Now are the Russians going to stand idly by and permit our tanks to roll in? Obviously not; they are going to shoot back. Reinforcements will be rushed up by both sides. Indeed, they will have already been moved up since our side would have had to prepare for the attack, while the Russian and German Communists will have observed our own build up (Berlin you understand being an *island inside Communist territory*) and will have matched or bettered it. Now has *National Review* magazine consulted the Berliners and Germans to see if *they* want war, at best tragic and at worst nuclear? Perhaps Mr. Goldwater's advisors have not thought matters through quite that far.

It may interest conservatives, in this connection, to know that I sometimes indulge in the creation of dramas in which I imagine myself in my opponent's shoes. Were I to picture myself in the position of Mr. Buckley, I might recommend for example the following—just to run it up the flagpole as they say: that the United States do everything in its power to eliminate nuclear weapons from the armories of the world, since all authorities agree that a full-scale nuclear war would simply result in mutual suicide for the engaged nations. And that on the very day the last A-bombs and H-bombs are dismantled, we initiate war with the Soviet Union and Communist China with *conventional* weapons. I think that to do so would be only slightly lesser folly than to become engaged in a nuclear war, but in any event there would be a certain consistency to such a policy and the acts flowing from it. Now to suppose that we could march across the vast face of the Asiatic mainland, mowing the enormous Chinese and Russian armies before us like wheat, is to suppose a great deal indeed. But at least we would be able to tell ourselves that we were engaging in this perculiar enterprise in an attempt to *liberate* Communist territory. Whereas when we recommend nuclear war—on China, on the Soviet Union—what we are talking about in terms of reality is not the *liberation* of the long suffering Russian and Chinese peoples, but their *incineration*. And when dealing with words like incineration, of course, one thinks of the tragic gap between the word—it comes easily out of the mouth—and the reality it is intended to convey.

I am no more afraid of death than is Mr. Buckley; it comes to us all, as he pointed out to us recently in an editorial. But I should not want to commit either murder or suicide.

William F. Buckley Jr.

Rebuttal:

MR. ALLEN presumably thought, at the beginning of his remarks, to rob me of the possibility of any authority in what I have to say by saying that after all, so rash am I that I oppose *the Pope himself*! Having read the autobiography of Mr. Allen, I was not aware that he respected the Pope's opinion on theological matters, let alone political matters. I suppose it deserves to get said, for the record (which record Mr. Allen did not see fit to introduce into the context of his remarks) that *National Review* is not a Catholic magazine. It is a magazine whose leadership I share with Protestants and with Jews and in point of fact with atheists. And it was our collective judgment, *not* that the Pope needs not to be taken seriously in the course of evaluating his encyclicals, but that in point of fact an encyclical issued to a waiting world in 1961 which sought to address itself to the major aspirations of the world and did not once *mention* the subject of Communism, would in the future, as we put it, *by some* be considered to be a venture in triviality. We were, of course, correct:

Obviously, for instance, it would be considered a venture in triviality by Cubans (who were much less interested in whether or not there should be agricultural subsidies than they were in the question whether or not Mass could be celebrated in Havana). And under the circumstances, I think it a pity that Mr. Allen sought to invoke the majesty of the Pope, for purposes highly tendentious, in an effort to show that the position adopted by myself and my colleagues is essentially irresponsible. This happens, have you noticed, to be the essence of his general charge. He manages, with wonderful geniality (which I so much admire and which I would like sometime to emulate), simultaneously to get inside the "democratic vibrations" between himself and the crowd, and also to condescend.

In effect, his argument tonight is based on experts. He is here, in effect, to say to us that, as a result of all of his reading, of all of his meditation on the subject, he understands our primitive impulses! But that the subject of foreign policy is of such an elusive complexity that we cannot begin to hope to understand it, that after all it is fit only for study by whomever is undertaking to do thirteen reports for a subcommittee of the Foreign Relations Committee of the United States Senate. We cannot cope with these problems, Mr. Allen says, simply by focusing our mere minds on the problems and coining such empty phrases as, "We want victory over Communism," coining such phrases presumably as, "Give me liberty, or give me death," coining such phrases as, for instance, that "We take these truths to be self-evident," which in fact tended to represent the moving force of American idealism at every critical juncture of American history . . . if Mr. Allen's point is as simple as this, and I *shudder* to think that it is, if it is as simple as to say that we cannot by a *mere act of will* cause the Soviet Union to go away, then let us instantly concede that point.

But if he wishes us, in effect, to say that as a result of the fact that we have not sat in on the deliberations between Senators Green and Fulbright and Wayne Morse on the Senate Foreign Relations Committee, we are not therefore equipped to understand the fact that Cuban freedom cannot be restored; that it was *absolutely* necessary for us to back Sukarno against those people in West Irian who wanted freedom; that it was *absolutely* necessary for us to send wheat to the Soviet Union when they asked for it; *absolutely* necessary for us to go right *to* the Bay of Pigs and then withdraw from it, then let me tell him something which will entitle him to think the worst of me. In all frankness, *I* would sooner (judging from the performances of the senators in question) have our foreign policy written by the Marx Brothers.

What *especially* struck me about the performance of Mr. Steve Allen was that he attempted, with his customary finesse, to lay tablet upon tablet in order to create the overarching structure on which he will repose his argument and his final conclusions. But the only thing that he said *effectively* tonight was "Shut up!" And when he did, he cut through, in my judgement quite properly, to something that needed to be said; because Mr. Steve Allen is here as a gentleman to share his platform with me, to do his best—as I am here to do my best—to present a competing point of view. And he was entitled to demand courtesy as a minor reciprocity for his kindness in coming. But all of a sudden, he took direct action. He didn't suggest to the moderator that this be referred to a committee in order to consider the psychological complexities involved.

I hasten to say that my own admiration of the penetrative power of the will and tenacity of Mr. Steve Allen is extraordinary. I sat as his guest two or three days ago at his studio and saw him with the most extraordinary equanimity, simultaneously in the course of one hour and a half without being ruffled in the least, preside over a show at which one woman wanted to show that she was the greatest bubble gum blower in the world, another three girls wanted to demonstrate that they had developed a new Twist in Chicago, Mr. Oleg Cassini wanted (within the bounds of what is permitted by the FCC) to demonstrate new foundation garments and Mr. Steve Allen undertook to fly like a batman on roller skates while pushed by a wind machine. A man who can schedule shows of *that* character four nights a week is hardly a man to be stayed by complexity (unless for some reason it has to do with foreign relations).

Let me repeat: the *besetting sin* of modern intellectuals, of which Mr. Allen is an unfortunate example, is ambiguity. What has happened in effect in our time, is that the nation has become convulsed as a result of its collision with certain philosophical trends which rob us of a sense of identity, and rob us of a sense of purpose, and rob us of *any idea that we are actually engaged in something that is worth doing for its own sake*. One has only to read the autobiography of Mr. Steve Allen to see how tormented he is by the groaning paradoxes of our time. And there is no question at all but that the kind of ambiguity that is represented in the deliberations of men like George Kennan, and men like Adlai Stevenson, and men like Professor Barghoorn (who has just returned from Soviet Russia) reflect this failure in America to come to grips with the essential question: namely, *Is this society worth defending at whatever is the necessary cost*?

It is perfectly easy to go to the library at Harvard University and look under "China, why it fell," and see two hundred volumes why it was "absolutely necessary" that it should go. By the same token, there will be apologies written for the "necessity" of the fall of South Viet Nam when that happens, of Laos when that happens, and the rest of it. And what has recently come (which causes Mr. Allen—who is primarily, philosophically ambiguous—great concern) is what he calls the "oversimplicity" of Mr. Goldwater; because Mr. Goldwater says that he wants victory over the Soviet Union. How, says he—incidentally rhetorically—is he going to accomplish this? Well, it is very carefully spelled out in 370 pages in a book by Mr. Goldwater that apparently Mr. Steve Allen would rather ridicule than read. But to the extent that he is alarmed by the prospect of a person who seeks the Presidency and who has no "program" for achieving victory over the Soviet Union, I recommend that book to him.

Now, actually, I think that the formulation "victory over the Soviet Union" is the improper one; it should rather be to "*neutralize* the Soviet threat"—because Mr. Allen is quite correct in suggesting that it is going to be impossible to have "victory over Communism" for so long as, hypothetically, a single person wishes to become a Communist. He is right in suggesting that such is the complexity of human nature and such the venality of so many human beings, that it is impossible to go out and wage the kind of mission that was attempted by for instance Woodrow Wilson (a great philosophical mentor of Mr. Allen) when he set out to make the world safe for democracy. No, we want, pending the successful completion of the objectives of the "Committee to Abolish Original Sin," not to convert all people from Communism, but to make it impossible for them to shatter our peace, to shatter our freedom. And it is the crowning responsibility—for which they shall have (I hope) to answer to a divine tribunal—it is the crowning blame of the liberal leadership of the past twelve or fifteen years that they may have made it possible for the enemy to have accumulated the power to "end (as Mr. Steve Allen puts it) life on this continent." No, the "complexity" is not the problem.

Mr. Allen, for instance, hasn't said what kind of "complexity" it was that caused Mr. Kennedy suddenly to draw back at the Bay of Pigs. Was it because he had read only twelve out of the thirteen projected studies of the Senate committee, and under the circumstances felt that he was not equipped to proceed with the operation? No, it was rather that fatal ambiguity which unfortunately is fed by people like Mr. Allen and his friends who are constantly talking about the apocalyptic horrors of nuclear war without understanding the essential realism of American foreign policy: which is, that it *rests* on the necessity for strength and the necessity for purpose. And that in the absence of the union of those two imperative qualities in our foreign policy, we will continue to lose our Cubas; we will continue to be humiliated in Berlin; we will continue to be surprised in India; we will continue to fail in Southeast Asia; we will continue to succumb to the drab, pusillanimous servilities of the Committee for a Sane Nuclear Policy.

And at *that*, simple though it is by contrast with the way Mr. Allen describes it, it is more complex than sometimes he assumes. Do you, he says rhetorically, know where Indonesia is? And you answer "Yes." He is transparently bowled over, and might in fact be bowled over by your answer to the questions:

Is there any rational reason for a Cuban to have any faith in American foreign policy?

Is there any rational reason for an Eastern European to have any faith in American foreign policy?

Or is there any rational reason for a Southeast Asian to have any faith in American foreign policy?

And, in fact, is there any rational reason to believe that in his entire eloquent but meandering statement Mr. Steve Allen made any kind of defense of our miserable policy of the last three years?

Steve Allen

Rebuttal:

Mr. Buckley has seen fit to imply that one who is not a Catholic cannot respect the social and moral commentaries of the Pope. In doing so he has offended first against logic, since the simple fact of the matter is that I do. And he has offended secondly against charity. I would like to think that this is uncharacteristic of him. I was moderately dismayed that Mr. Buckley would introduce a note of that sort into the exchange, but more so by his apparent willingness to appropriate to himself (and to his political counterparts) the Constitution of the United States, the American flag and Almighty God. I had been under the impression until that moment that we all held these in common. My blood races at the same rate as Mr. Buckley's, at phrases such as "We take these truths to be self-evident," such phrases as "Give me liberty, or give me death." And I stand shoulder to shoulder with him in absolutely insisting that this society and our way of life is worth defending at all costs. And therefore I am entitled to resent his inferences to the contrary.

Now as I have suggested, there are two ways, generally speaking, of looking at the subject matter of this evening's discussion. One question, which we've already taken up, is: how good is what might loosely be described (since this thing does go back, you know) as the Truman-Eisenhower-Kennedy foreign policy—how good has it been? The other question is: how good is the foreign policy with which today's conservatives would replace our present policies? We must, I'm sure Mr. Buckley would agree, deal with both these questions. For if you do nothing more than criticize our present foreign policy, you're going only half way, if that. The most effective political criticism, unfortunately, is almost always vague. If the voters respond favorably to your emotional tone, if you tell them often enough to throw the rascals out, they may well usher you into office (even if they do not clearly know the nature of the beast that you recommend they mount).

I told you earlier that conservatives are invariably annoyed, if not infuriated, by references to Goldwater's simplistic approach to complex problems. And if the point is not particularly important coming from me, perhaps you will not mind my quoting Mr. John Foster Dulles, who wrote this: "Those who are most positive about political problems are able to be postive only because they do not know all the relevant facts. There are no longer any simple problems," Mr. Dulles said, "nor any easy solutions." But I do not mean to suggest that either Mr. Goldwater or Mr. Buckley have failed to give us *any* specific alternatives. They indeed have, which Mr. Buckley has brought to your attention. Let's take up, therefore, some of these particulars.

Contrary to what some of their more hot-headed followers suppose, many responsible conservatives share with liberals the opinion that one of the primary objectives of American foreign policy must be the *prevention* of nuclear war. Neither conservatives nor liberal leaders, however, have maintained that nuclear war must be avoided at all costs. Now let's get this very straight! If the Soviet Union this evening were to present us with the strictly limited choice between nuclear war and surrender, the response, as everyone knows perfectly well, would be to decide in favor of war—which is why the Soviet Union will present us with no such choice. Therefore, many conservatives and liberals conclude, we must develop techniques necessary to counter Communist aggression within the context of the present nuclear stalemate. Now you might suppose that a favorite right-wing alternative would be the one recommended by General Maxwell Taylor (among others), that we prepare for limited or non-nuclear war. But surprisingly enough, this is not acceptable to the right, according to M. Stanton Evans, writing in *National Review*, January 29, 1963: "Confronted by our atomic arsenal," he says, "the Soviets are not likely to send their armies marching across borders. In the assumed condition of nuclear deadlock, the more probable form of aggression is 'sublimited'—guerrilla action, the capture of nationalist movements, subversion." And, no doubt feeling under pressure to be specific, Mr. Evans spelled out the required counter measures: the helicopter airlift of troops and strategic village tactics employed in South Viet Nam. Well now, it is immediately apparent Mr. Evans has led us down the garden path which has curved full circle, for these are precisely the tactics already being employed by armed forces operating under a Commander in Chief who is a member of the hated liberal establishment.

Do not suppose, by the way, that spokesmen of the right feel the least bit comfortable in the arena of mutual nuclear deterrents. For this situation, Mr. Evans and his colleagues tell us, does not deter the Communists; it deters only us. "We are prevented," he says, "from bombing north of the

Yalu River or helping Hungarian freedom fighters because such action might 'touch off a nuclear holocaust.' The Communists," he continues, "are not prevented from subverting Laos or the Congo or Cuba." Now, Mr. Evans is confusing us, possibly because he is confused himself. Let's see if I can make this clear to you. He opposes an entity identified as "we" on the one hand, to an entity identified as "the Communists" on the other. So let's try to identify the "we," and try to identify "the Communists." By "we" he means the armed forces of the United States. But it's not so easy to determine what he means when he says "the Communists." He cannot possibly mean the armed forces of the Soviet Union, since Russian troops have *not* been responsible for subverting Laos, or Cuba, or the Congo, or Viet Nam. No, unfortunately the Communists we are talking about (damn the complexity of it all!) are a combination of native Communists and foreign revolutionaries. It's therefore nonsense to pretend that there is some sort of balanced choice between the activities of the United States Army on the one hand, and, for example, the peasant supporters of Fidel Castro on the other. Now when we speak in large generalizations about those we call a–the Communists, and b–the armed forces of the Soviet Union, we must get it through our heads that the two, though obviously related, are distinct entities.

To give but one example of the ways in which failure to make this basic distinction confuses us, consider the right-wing argument one sometimes hears to the effect that though a nuclear war would be an ultimate horror (which no one denies), at least by wiping the Soviet Union off the map—or at the very least destroying the bulk of its armed forces—we would thereby put an end to Communism. Would that it were so. But the claim is absurd. To begin with, Communism is essentially an *idea*—perhaps the most evil idea the mind of man has ever conceived. It exists, unfortunately, in the minds of millions of people who are not Russian at all. So what would actually happen, in the full-scale nuclear war that some critics of the administration are able calmly to contemplate, is not the destruction of Communism but a—the destruction of the Soviet Union (with, remember, its largely innocent and non-Communist populations), and b—the destruction of the United States (after which isolated Communist infection spots all over the world would be able to breed and flourish anew, feeding on the chaos of war and having no longer to worry about the retaliatory power—military, economic or moral—of the United States). And such belligerent nonsense, if you please, is invariably considered by those who are forever demanding an *offensive* strategy.

Such particulars of strategy are indeed offensive: offensive to common sense, offensive to the Judaeo-Christian moral tradition, offensive to human dignity, and offensive to our national security.

It's been brought to your attention this evening that I am affiliated with the National Committee for a Sane Nuclear Policy, an organization which has devoted its efforts chiefly to informing the American people of the realities and implications of the nuclear arms race. For some reason, our conservative brethren seem to be infuriated when we point out that full-scale nuclear war is immoral; and that it would result in widespread death and suffering today, and untold genetic tragedy for the unhappy generations to come. Now this is important: these assertions are never denied, they are *never* denied; it's just that they make the warhawks squirm uncomfortably. Very well gentlemen, if you will not listen to SANE, will you listen to General David M. Shoup, Commandant of the United States Marines, who has predicted time and again that a full-scale nuclear war will cause 700 to 800 million deaths? He correctly points out, by the way (and this is a fascinating point to be considered by, first of all, every man—with special interest to our southern conservatives), that the great majority of these deaths would be suffered by members of the white race, and therefore concludes that for all practical purposes, the white race would be finished on this planet by a nuclear war of such a magnitude. So, when it comes to planning with such matters, we may not really be dealing so much with "policy" as with lunacy and absurdity.

Or again, gentlemen, if you will not listen to SANE, will you listen to Pope John XXIII, who has said the following: "It is with deep sorrow that we note the enormous stocks of armaments that have been and still are being made in more economically developed countries, with a vast outlay of intellectual and economic resources. And so it happens that while the people of these countries are loaded with heavy burdens, other countries as a result are deprived of the collaboration they need in order to make economic and social progress. The production of arms is allegedly justified on the grounds that in present day conditions, peace cannot be preserved without an equal balance of armaments. And so, if one country increases its armaments, others feel the need to do the same. And if one country is equipped with nuclear weapons, other countries must produce their own, equally destructive. People live in constant fear, lest the storm that every moment threatens should break upon them with dreadful violence; and with good reason, for the arms of war are ready at hand. It cannot be denied that the conflagration may be set off by some uncontrollable and unexpected change. It is to be feared," the Pope concludes, "that the mere continuance of nuclear tests, undertaken with war in mind, will have fatal consequences for life on earth. Justice then, right reason and humanity urgently demand that the arms race should cease, that the stockpiles which exist in various countries should be reduced equally and simultaneously by the parties concerned, that *nuclear weapons should be banned*, and that a general agreement should eventually be reached, about progressive disarmament and an effective method of control. In the words of Pius XII, our predecessor of happy memory, 'The calamity of a world war, with the economic and social ruin and the moral excesses and dissolution that accompany it, must not be permitted to envelop the human race for a third time.' " That's the end of the Pope's statement.

Another point which I wish to make very clear is that the National Committee for a Sane Nuclear Policy does *not* recommend unilateral nuclear disarmament. It supports the longstanding, *American* principle of phased mutual disarmament controlled by inspection. I personally see very little likelihood of greater progress being made at the present time. (And this, of course, is an enormously complicated area, fraught with—as Mr. Buckley has pointed out—ambiguities and dangers. But the general outlines of a sound policy are distinguishable.)

Lastly, if you will not listen to SANE, will you listen to General of the Army, Douglas MacArthur, who has written: "The tremendous evolution of nuclear and other potentials of destruction has suddenly taken the problem of war away from its primary consideration as a moral and spiritual question and brought it abreast of scientific realism. It is no longer an ethical question to be pondered solely by learned philosophers and ecclesiastics, but a hard core one, for the decision of the masses whose survival is the issue. Many will tell you," General MacArthur concludes, "with mockery and ridicule, that the abolition of war can only be a dream, that it is but the vague imagining of a visionary. But we must go on toward the goal of peace or we will go under."

Now, just quickly, a few words on *Cuba*. Conservatives tell us daily that the administration (and it was Republican, remember) and the State Department were remiss, to say the least, in not recognizing Fidel Castro for the Marxist that he eventually proved to be. Concerning this, a number of things need to be said.

First, the mistake about Castro was made by practically our entire people. Mr. Buckley might blame *The New York Times*, but all of us have to share some of that blame, I believe.

Second, the CIA (which until this evening I was not aware was a liberal organization) must have been party to the error.

Third, there was available, evidently, information about Castro's Marxist background in his college days, but this could have proved nothing about his present sympathies (for the reason that many a man who was a college Communist leaves the Party when he becomes better informed and more mature). Some of Mr. Buckley's best friends, as the saying goes, are former Communists. There were, it seems reasonable to assume, a few who raised their voices from the very first to call Castro a Communist. Unfortunately, some of these voices had cried "Wolf" too long to be taken seriously. Those who later told us that Dwight and Milton Eisenhower and John Foster Dulles and Charles de Gaulle, among others, were Communists can scarcely suppose that such credentials establish their rating as reliable political prophets.

Fourth, the most important point of all, the crime of those Americans who were taken in by Castro assumes somewhat smaller proportions when we consider that many of the Cuban freedom fighters, who now live in Florida, were once Castro's staunchest supporters and right hand men. They were with him all the way, in the mountains, in the villages; and their suspicions were not aroused. Now, it seems to me that there is definite evidence of hypocrisy in the conservative criticism of Fidel Castro on the grounds that he turned out to be a Marxist. For such criticism implies that if he had *not* been a Marxist, but only a liberal agrarian reformer, then conservatives would have joined the American majority in welcoming him. Nothing could be further from the truth! Conservatives were against him, *whatever* he was, simply because he proposed to do something about the disgraceful economic injustice under which the Cuban people had suffered for so many years. His right-wing critics were actually *overjoyed* when it became possible to accurately describe him as a Communist.

Now, criticism of the fact that we did not provide air cover for the Bay of Pigs invasion force labors under the invalid assumption that the invasion would have been a certain success if air cover had been provided. I know of no evidence to substantiate this. While I would be every bit as gratified as Mr. Buckley would if Fidel Castro would suddenly disappear in a puff of smoke, I am nevertheless forced to take into consideration that a great many Cubans, unhappily, still support Fidel Castro. And even more supported him two years ago when the invasion attempt occurred. It was comparatively easy to overthrow Batista because he was a widely despised tyrant and murderer, corrupt in both his personal and political capacity. His power came from the machine guns of his army and from the cordial support of the United States. But Fidel Castro came to power on a wave of the most enthusiastic popular support. That his revolution has in many respects gone sour is apparent to the proverbial six-year-old child.

We don't need any conservative advice to tell us that! But, evidently many Cubans still consider themselves better off than they were formerly and so are content to go along with the present regime. It may well be, therefore, that those who hope for a popular anti-Castro uprising in Cuba are deluding themselves. I very much hope not, but it would be presumptuous of me to assert that my hopes necessarily reflect the political realities.

All the real experts on Latin America agree that Castro is merely a symptom of the dread economic disease that afflicts Latin American nations. It can scarcely be maintained by any fair minded man that a system whereby the overwhelming majority of the people are poverty stricken and a tiny minority are incredibly wealthy is just one. But as far as Senator Goldwater can see, the answer to Fidel Castro is not American support for a profound democratic social revolution, but rather the mere rolling up of sleeves and the landing of American troops in Cuba.

Steve Allen

Conclusion:

CONSERVATIVES ARE entirely correct in pointing out that liberals have made mistakes, but the reason is not that they are liberals but that they are human beings. Conservatives over the years have made their share of mistakes, and if fewer have been observable it's simply because they have less frequently held positions of power. One example: in the issue of *National Review*, December 3, 1960, the editors complimented themselves on the fact that in November of that year, the magazine had published a special supplement, edited by James Burnham, in which eight of the world's leading geopoliticians detailed why no split between Russia and Red China was likely, though liberal commentators had long pointed to the possibility. Now if eight of the world's leading geopoliticians were wrong about this (as they obviously were), then it is small wonder that we lesser mortals are from time to time mistaken.

Those who would light the torch of war now are not only closing their own minds to future possibilities: they would take it upon themselves to deny the rest of us the right to live out the human adventure in all its constructive potential. Asserting our right to the simple continuing projection of human history would seem to involve making the barest minimum demand, but there are a few among us who seem to question even that right. Now our conservative advisers frequently tell us that we ought not to give military or economic assistance to nations that are not fervently committed to the side of freedom, as Mr. Nixon has put it. At first glance there might seem to be some merit to this idea, but when it's applied to actual cases, one realizes again the danger of naive approaches to complicated, sophisticated problems.

A basic question here, of course, is exactly what countries are meant when we refer to nations that are not "firmly committed to the side of freedom" (and do we really mean freedom or only anti-Communism?). Now, if we're talking about, say, Yugoslavia or Poland, the issue may be at least relatively unambiguous. But if we are referring to the uncommitted nations, then the advice of our conservative brethren may be dangerous because it could mean cutting off aid to neutral countries from whom we could eventually work some advantage.

And what of the Western nations of today's world that are firmly committed to one degree of socialization or another? Conservatives tell us that socialism is slavery, that it is flatly opposed to freedom. Therefore, according to conservative logic, the Scandinavian nations, for example, are not firmly committed to the side of freedom. Would Mr. Goldwater perhaps eventually go so far as to refuse to engage in political dialogue with them too?

Or let us be dramatic and suppose that the argument between China and the Soviet Union eventually leads to an outbreak of hostilities between the two powers—there's no immediate prospect of that happening but we don't know what the future will bring (at the end of this century half the people on this planet will be Chinese). Now would we then be willing to give military aid to one side or another?

We damn well might, for it might serve our own interests. After all, during the Second World War we gave an enormous amount of military equipment to the Soviet Union, despite the deep mutual distrust between the two nations, simply because we knew that the business at hand was the defeat of the Nazi and Fascist powers.

Now our conservative critics have every right to be dismayed, as is every intelligent human being, by the threat that Communism poses to the world. But they have no right to suppose or insinuate that our leaders are secretly sympathetic to Communism, or that they are totally uninformed about the realities of the situation, or that they lack courage.

I must say, in conclusion, that I see something enormously comic—as well as tragic—about a man with Mr. Goldwater's intellectual credentials in effect telling Walter Lippmann or President Kennedy or Dean Rusk or Senator Fulbright that they just don't understand the business of conducting foreign relations. Now when right-wing foreign policy alternatives are distilled to their essence, we find that they consist of exactly two substances: one involves our committing acts of war, and the other involves simply quitting (childishly walking off the field, ending foreign aid, abandoning the United Nations, withdrawing our representatives from any nation that displeases us and sulking in the corner while the march of history sweeps past us). Both alternatives—and I use the word with the utmost precision—are *un-American*. The United States has always been a peaceful nation, though its people are mighty when attacked. And the American people have never been quitters; nor, I am confident, will they be now.

William F. Buckley Jr.

Conclusion:

For the record, I want to get this pope stuff straight. I did *not* imply that someone who is not a Catholic should not respect a statement of the Pope, unless "respecting a statement of the Pope"—which is something Catholics do because they feel the distinct possibility that a statement from the Pope may under certain circumstances have God as its provenance—means simply discovering in it a similarity to one's own, pre-established political views. For instance, when the socialist *Manchester Guardian* proclaimed the arrival of a new socialist Pope on earth at the moment when *Mater et Magistra* was promulgated, it seemed to me anomalous that the editors of the *Manchester Guardian* were showing such deep reverence for the wisdom of a man who is after all the chief figure in a religion which said editors believe, most of them, to be merely the dregs of religious superstition. I don't mind at all Mr. Steve Allen quoting popes when he wants to. But I do wish he would quote more representative statements of them. The popes are, of course, and have proved themselves consistently to be, the most implacable enemies of Communism that exist on this earth. It was

Pope Pius XII, whom Mr. Allen refers to as of "blessed memory," who said that anyone who co-operated with the Communists in any enterprise whatsoever was excommunicated from the Catholic Church.

Now having got through *that,* let me just say that Mr. Allen's confusion is not unique. That is to say, that although he is here (as he has told us twice) representing himself only, his confusion is a shared confusion. And under the circumstances he does belong intimately to the fraternity of foreign policy makers which we are here to examine tonight.

I do not know how it is possible to correct or to try to amplify to a man whose idea of Cuba is as is Mr. Allen's idea of Cuba; who, for instance, will tell you that the reason why Communism exists in Cuba is as a sort of reaction to the days of Batista, when in point of fact, despicable though Batista was, he in fact did preside over a country in which there was dissent, in which there was freedom of opposition in the press, in which occasionally there were elections, in which in fact the economic standard of life was high. And there is no doubt in my mind that ninety-eight per cent of the Cuban people today, if given the horrible choice between Castro and Batista, would instantly choose Batista. Cuba was, under Batista, the second richest country per capita in Latin America and this included the people and not merely the gamblers, "most of whom were American exploiters," and the rest of it. Let's not turn this into a question of "Ought we all to despise Batista?" My credentials go back rather earlier that those of the left wing, whose hero he was, you may remember, for many years before they decided that he had betrayed them in 1957.

Now, how can one discuss these matters with a man so confused. A man who says of Algeria that Algeria is

merely a "kind of socialist state"—and more or less implies that Suzanne Labin (a socialist) and Sidney Hook
(a socialist) would not find very much to quarrel with
contemporary Algeria about. (Suzanne Labin and Sidney
Hook endorse most fervently the anti-Communist foreign
policy described over the years in *National Review,* I am
proud to say). How can one edge forward to an understanding of what is going on when Mr. Steve Allen simply
refuses to acknowledge that something of great dramatic
moment happened at the Bay of Pigs, when a liberation
movement that had been planned was suddenly withdrawn.
He insists that, after all, everybody, or more or less everybody, in the Sane Nuclear Policy Committee is absolutely
agreed on the proposition that if necessary we will use a
nuclear force in order to prevent the takeover of the world
by the Soviet Union. But he is absolutely and flatly wrong.
One third, for instance, of the student body of Harvard
University has said in a recent poll (*one third*) that they
would sooner surrender to the Soviet Union that fight a
nuclear war; and a substantial portion of that third belongs
to the Committee for a Sane Nuclear Policy. I was there
at Hunter College when I saw young girls embracing each
other, expecting not to see themselves again the next day,
because Mr. Kennedy had just gone on the air giving an
ultimatum to the Soviet Union to withdraw its missiles
from Cuba.

Such is the kind of emotional confusion that it represents, in my judgment, a syndrome. The reason why the
Committee for a Sane Nuclear Policy (though it may not
in some of its crystallizations be shown to be ambiguous on
the point of "Give me liberty or give me death") is a mis-
chievous force in American affairs—the kind of force that
is always there, incapacitating and paralyzing the Execu-
tive Department of this country—is because it is obsessed

with the idea of the bomb. I once debated with Mr. Norman Cousins on foreign policy and he spent the first fifteen minutes describing graphically, as Mr. Steve Allen has done in fewer minutes, the terrible ravages of the bomb if one fell here, how far would it spread over, how many people would it kill and so on. . . . I remember that my mind tended to wander after absolutely establishing that the hottest blast, if it fell on the Battery, would reach to *The New York Times* building. But the kind of obsessiveness with the bomb, the kind of willingness to believe that it was the "economic misery of Cuba that caused Castro," the kind of willingness to believe that the United Nations is a *deus ex machina, that* is what in fact incapacitates not only Mr. Allen but the President of the United States from waging effective policy.

Says he, how dare we, in effect (referring to his original theme), criticize men like Rusk, men like Lippmann, men like Fulbright? Mr. Lippmann was back there applauding Mussolini 30 years ago, in the early stages of his punditry, and telling us we had nothing whatever to fear from Hitler. Rusk was telling us in 1951 that the time had probably come to recognize that we couldn't hang on to the offshore islands. Mr. Fulbright has compiled an obstinate record of derelictions which are very hard even, I should think, for *Mrs.* Fulbright to defend, let alone Mr. Allen

So what we do have is a syndrome, and I conclude by simply stating one simple thing: if we cannot yet recognize a foreign policy, which over a period of fifteen years has resulted in the Soviet Union's accumulating the strength to destroy us, all at the will of a single individual, then we have not begun to learn the necessity for reexamining our premises and doing something before it is too late.

Robert M. Hutchins

vs.

L. Brent Bozell

The Supreme Court

"Resolved: The 1954 decision on school
integration should be supported."

Robert M. Hutchins

Opening Statement:

I WISH FIRST explicitly to deny that I am about
to present a liberal viewpoint, or any other partisan viewpoint. If I am presenting a viewpoint, it is what I regard
as a conservative viewpoint. That is, I regard the decision
of the Court in Brown *vs.* Board of Education as in the
orthodox, received tradition of American jurisprudence.
I do not regard it as a departure from the past, or the habits
of the Court in the past, or the conception that the Court
or the people have had of the Court's function. I regard
it, I say, as in the received and in the best tradition of
American jurisprudence.

The essence of a community is learning together. And
a political community arises when the citizens are learning together how to achieve the good of the community
and how to govern themselves. A democratic political
community arises when all the people are citizens. A
democratic community has as its constitution a charter of
learning. That is what our Constitution is. We the people
are continuously to learn how to form a more perfect
union, how to promote the common defense, domestic
tranquility, how to establish justice and how to preserve

the blessings of liberty for ourselves and our posterity.

This was the view of the Court taken by the first great chief justice, Mr. Chief Justice Marshall, who kept saying, "We must never forget that it is a constitution that we are interpreting." This, I suppose, is the single most quoted statement that Mr. Chief Justice Marshall ever made. It is quoted by justices on every issue in almost every important case. And what it is thought to mean is that the Constitution is a living document. It is a charter of learning. It can almost be said that the only case in which this doctrine was forgotten was the Dred Scott Case, where Mr. Chief Justice Taney held that the precise words of the Founders must be interpreted in the precise conditions under which they lived; and since under the conditions under which they lived the Negro had no rights that a white man was bound to respect, the Negro had, at the date of the Dred Scott decision, no rights that a white man was bound to respect.

Contrast that with the position taken by Mr. Chief Justice Hughes in the celebrated Blaisdell Case, in which he said that we are here not to execute the ideas of the Founders as though conditions had not changed since the Founders lived; we are here to execute the ideas of the Founders, recognizing the changes that have occurred. And the decision that we are about to make in this case, he says, "is the flower of the seeds that the Fathers planted."

I do not know anybody who dissents from the proposition that *stare decisis,* the doctrine that precedent is binding on succeeding cases, is inapplicable to constitutional decisions. The Constitution is always open to reinterpretation because it is a charter of learning.

In the process of learning in which a democratic political community must engage, in the process of learning in which *this* democratic political community must engage, the Supreme Court has been singled out by our history, if not by the express words of the Constitution, as the guardian of our principles and as the interpreter of our goals.

Now the Fourteenth Amendment provides that no state may deny any person the equal protection of the laws. And we today have to find out what this means, under the changing conditions of our lives, in the light of such knowledge as we now possess and in the light of the history we have experienced.

The doctrine of Plessy *vs.* Ferguson in 1896 is a doctrine that wormed its way backwards into American jurisprudence insofar as education, and the process of education, has been affected by it. Plessy *vs.* Ferguson was a case of public accommodations, and the Court referred to the general practice of segregation at that day, in education, in order to back up its holding that the state could, if it wished, provide separate but equal accomodations in public accomodations for Negroes and whites. Plessy *vs.* Ferguson, as I say, came in by the back door. The doctrine of Brown *vs.* Board of Education, however, comes in by the front door, after 16 years of litigation affecting the rights of Negroes as they bear on the duties of the state to provide educational opportunities for them, and it is decided explicitly on this issue by a unanimous Court.

Now when we ask, What does the Fourteenth Amendment mean, in talking about equal protection of the laws? of course it is not contended that a child is denied equal protection because he is compelled to go to school when an adult is not. Justice involves treating unequals unequally. Therefore, the Supreme Court has always held that the states may make reasonable classifications among their citizens, and the only question in Brown *vs.* Board of Education is whether color is a reasonable basis of legal classification by a state. The Court holds, and I think correctly, that "separate but equal" has turned out to be a bad joke.

The Court held that color was not a reasonable basis of

classification. The Attorneys General of the United States, representing both parties in the Truman and in the Eisenhower administrations, took the same view. And one who differs with Brown *vs*. Board of Education must argue that color is a reasonable basis of discrimination by a state among its citizens. (I assume that it will not be argued that a classification is reasonable because a state legislature says it is.)

The power of judicial review of state laws was established by the First Judiciary Act and has never, so far as I know, been questioned since. The adherents of the status quo were the chief supporters of judicial review, not merely of state legislation but also of congressional legislation, from 1865 to 1937, and the supporters of the status quo cannot now deny the power because they do not like the way it is exercised.

I assume that it will not be argued that the classification proposed in the segregation of schools is reasonable because the Negro is inherently inferior. On this point certainly we have learned better. And what the Court points out in Brown *vs*. Board of Education is that we have learned a good deal. In 1896, when Plessy *vs*. Ferguson was decided, public education was not an important activity in this country. Only one southern state, Kentucky, even had a compulsory education law. Education was a pleasant sort of diversion for the people who could afford it; it was not regarded as the indispensable foundation of our liberties. Nor was it regarded as the indispensable foundation of the individual's economic achievement. Education I will not say was irrelevant in 1896, but it clearly did not have that importance in the life of our society and in the life of the individual which it has now assumed.

I believe that the only way in which Brown *vs*. Board of

Education can be successfully attacked is to argue that when the people of a state want to make their prejudices about color the basis of their society, they may do so in spite of the provisions of the Fourteenth Amendment and the generous intentions of the Preamble of the Constitution of the United States. And they do so because they are prejudiced. But this is to erect prejudice into a constitutional principle, and this is to deny the spirit, if not the letter, of the Constitution and to reject it as a charter of learning.

It seems to me that on certain matters we have to have a national policy. We have a federal system, but we have to have a national policy on certain matters. One such question is, Who is a citizen? The Negro clearly is. The second such question is, What are the rights of citizens? It seems to me that it must be held, in the process of learning under our Constitution, that all the citizens of the United States must everywhere be treated with common decency and humanity, and that they must have access to all public facilities.

In recent years the Court has totally changed the rules of criminal procedure which I used to teach years ago. Years ago it was held that there was a federal rule and there were state rules, on everything from forced confessions to assistance of counsel to indigent defendants—anything you like. The state could do what it chose. The federal rule might be totally different. This has now been changed, and I think it has been changed in recognition of this simple principle: on certain matters we must have a national policy. And our national policy about the treatment of criminals or those alleged to be criminals must be one that conforms to our national view of due process of law. And so it is with the Negro.

It seems to me, then, that to oppose the decision of the

court in Brown *vs.* Board of Education is to argue for the perpetuation of the shame of America. It is a hundred years since Emancipation. The crime of slavery was a white crime. The crime of Reconstruction was a white crime. The treatment of the Negro that followed from these two crimes is the greatest crime of all.

It is time to put an end to it, and the way to do so is to declare that no government in this country may discriminate among its citizens on the basis of their color. The Constitution is color blind, and this the Supreme Court has now held.

L. Brent Bozell

Opening Statement:

I THINK IT is testimony, probably, to the success of the conservative cause that the spokesman for the point of view you have just heard should see fit to sail under the conservative banner.

Dr. Hutchins has spent a lifetime promoting learning and has caused a great number of people to profit from his endeavors. One of his most famous achievements is *The Great Books,* as you may know. I have not myself used my *Syntopicon* (the book that you use to find out how to use the volumes) to discover where it is one goes to look for definitions of constitutions. But I suggest that wherever one looks, from Plato to Freud, one will not find constitutions defined as "charters of learning." They are more frequently known as charters of government. And I should like us tonight to examine the potential of the American Constitution as a charter of government and to ask ourselves what loyalty we as citizens of the United States *owe* to it as a charter of government.

And let me at the outset register a hope that may strike many of you as unfeeling and frivolous (and perhaps others more sympathetic, as forlorn); and that is that those

73

around the country who are responsible for conducting the public discussion process will begin to regard the school desegregation decision of 1954 as worth discussing not so much because of the problems it raises about the issue of race relations, but because of the problems it raises precisely in the area of constitutional morality. And in all events, I shall do my best to point tonight's discussion in that direction. I say "my best" because, of course, there are two of us in the debate, and from here on out Dr. Hutchins may want to push it in another direction—and as we all know, Dr. Hutchins' best is perenially very good indeed.

Let me right off then, by way of getting a couple of points out of the way, make a confession of personal bias —as a matter of fact, two of them. First, I confess to approving the integration of public schools provided the local community concerned has also registered its approval; which is only to say that I would hope for integration in any community in which I might live. And the second is merely a corollary to my proviso, namely that I oppose the forcible imposition of integration on local communities that do not approve of it. And in professing these biases, I do not mean to suggest that the *problems* they involve are one dimensional, that they are to be solved merely by invoking the ideal of local democracy (any more than that they are to be solved merely by invoking the ideal of justice for Negroes). I *do* mean to say, however, that the issues they raise are not nearly so important as the issue the Supreme Court raised in the Brown Case, and in other cases decided under a similar theory of jurisprudence— the issue, namely, of whether a majority of that Court can, or should try to, alter the fundamental political structure under which our society lives.

And if the objection be interposed, at this early stage,

that constitutional niceties are not, after all, to be weighed on the same scales as what our learned commentators call "human problems," let me now make still a third confession. I believe that the alleged dichotomy between the integrity of the political process and compassion for human beings is the invention of demagogues, and is false. I believe that this side of Revelation, the successful solution of human problems presupposes not so much an agreement about what the solutions are, as an agreement about how solutions are to be sought. The society that is successful in solving human problems is the one that has committed itself to a *method* of policy making—of identifying its goals, of adjusting its differences, of forming its consensuses—that is in keeping with its own ethos, its own genius, its own traditions. And above all, it is a society whose members, having an understanding of those commitments, are prepared to honor them equally when immediate self-interest is served as when it is not—are willing, in a word, to play by the rules of the game. This is what I mean by "constitutional morality."

And I hasten to point out the obvious: that the most conspicuous beneficiaries of morality are not majorities but minorities. Majorities, if it is not for morality, can have their way by force of numbers or by force of superior power, but minorities, after morality has broken down, are normally at the mercy of brute power. And if I could think of advice that might be useful to minorities who suppose they may have profited from recent transgressions and perversions of our constitutional morality—the leftist agitators who have defied our security laws, the atheists who have succeeded in preventing school children from praying, the Negroes who have had doors opened to them by federal bayonets—I would remind them that the patience of majorities is finite. The Supreme Court orders they now wave in our faces are *ultimately* no more valid and will ultimately claim no more respect than the constitional morality that has given the orders such legitimacy as they possess. And let the Court itself flout the constitutional order, and let it do so over a period of time, as a matter of deliberate policy as this Court has done; and let our learned commentators, pretending not to see the transgression, egg the mischief-makers on; *then* the day is not far when this heretofore prudent and peaceful society will have learned to resolve its differences by will and main force.

I have, then, two principal points to make: the *first* is that in the Brown Case, the Supreme Court did not honor its obligation to apply the Constitution to the facts presented to it, and so itself violated the Constitution. And my *second* point is that those among us who, perceiving the illegitimacy of the Court's command, nonetheless insist that it be obeyed, are not only compounding the evil of that particular case, but are undermining the integrity of the constitutional order which all of us are obliged to uphold.

Now the decision itself is typically defended either on the grounds that the intentions of the framers of the Constitution were unclear on the question of segregated schools, or on the grounds that their intentions don't matter much anyway. It has been clear from what we have heard tonight that Dr. Hutchins rather prefers the second ground. He devoted not a moment at all of his address to the question of what the people who wrote the Fourteenth Amendment might have had in their minds. He went on to tell us that the concern of the Warren Court, as indeed it was, was primarily to look upon modern American society and to decide what was best for it. But as I have said a little earlier, aside from our legitimate hesitation to confer upon the present Chief Justice and his colleagues the right to decide what is best for the American society, aside from *that,* it seems to me that we ought to pay a *little* more attention to what might be meant by a constitution.

I take it that it is not simply a blank check, written out to future Supreme Courts, to be filled out according to the designs those Supreme Courts regard to be in the public interest. If it were, I can think of a form of words in which to frame such a constitution. They would go much like, "We the People ordain this Constitution as an instrument which the Supreme Court will cite when it wants to change American society."

But, by and large, constitutional scholars have regarded the intentions of the people who wrote the document with some respect. They have understood that if the constitutional principle is to have any meaning at all, it must mean that a prior generation binds a future generation to a certain course of action until that future generation, *through certain stipulated procedures,* chooses to change the rules that were earlier imposed. If this is not a correct picture of a constitution, if it is antiquated and no longer fit for study at the Center for the Study of Democratic Institutions, then Dr. Hutchins will surely tell us about that. But in the meantime, I am going to assume that there is some legitimacy in looking into what the framers of the Fourteenth Amendment meant to do. And my point about the Fourteenth Amendment is not that it had a point of view on segregated schools or the desegregation of schools; my point about the framers of the Fourteenth Amendment is that they had no view at all on education. At least they did not attempt to incorporate any such view in the document they wrote.

It has been said, over and over again, that you cannot run a society on the basis of the knowledge of people who

weren't familiar with the problems that confront us now.
Well, the framers of the Fourteenth Amendment were
roughly familiar with the problems that confront us now.
There were then white people. There were then black
people. There were then schools. There were then public
schools. There were some few integrated ones and there
were lots of segregated ones. And consequently, the opportunity for them to look at this problem was altogether
there. And the question I suggest that we might be interested in is, What did they do about it? And the answer
that all of the documentation affords—and it is documentation that is attested to not only by my kind of conservative but Dr. Hutchins' kind of conservative (those who
have given it any study at all)—is that education was
simply not included within the scope of the amendment.

What the amendment was designed to do was to give
constitutional sanction to the Civil Rights Act of 1866.
And that act, as you may know, dealt primarily with the
problem of how to make recently emancipated Negroes
what we might call "legal persons." And as a result, the
act, in the first instance, said something like that. But then
some of its proponents said, "If you are vague in the
language, you might get into the problem of social rights.
People might think it applies to schools." And at that
point, Representative Wilson of Iowa, who was chairman
of the Judiciary Committee to which the bill was committed, made this comment about the things covered by
this act. He said, "Do they mean in all things civil, social,
political, all citizens without distinction of race or color
shall be equal? By no means can they be so construed. Nor
do they mean that their children shall attend the same
schools. These are not civil rights or immunities." But beyond that, the proponents of the act thought it wise to
stipulate just what they *did* mean, and consequently they

made *this* the language of the act: that "citizens of every race and color shall have the same rights—to make and enforce contracts, to sue, to be parties, to give evidence, to inherit, purchase, lease, sell, hold and convey real and personal property and to full and equal benefit of all laws and proceedings for the security of persons and property —as enjoyed by white citizens."

Now that was the reach of the Civil Rights Act, and the very same Congress that passed that act a few months later proposed the Fourteenth Amendment. And not a single word was uttered in the halls of Congress during these debates suggesting that the amendment applied in any way at all to education. And that is not all. That same Congress *did* pass a law expressly establishing schools exclusively for colored children in the city of Georgetown within the District of Columbia, and I cannot imagine more conclusive evidence that nothing was further from the minds of the proposers of that amendment than that it would apply to schools or that it would exclude segregated schools.

And the same picture is evident if you look at the records of the state conventions that ratified the amendment. In state after state (we can talk about the details later on if you like) there is evidence of two things. Either the state which ratified the amendment already had a segregated school system and went right on having it, or the state in question did not have such a system but went ahead and established one, two or three years after the amendment was passed. And there were some northern states with relatively negligible Negro populations which had no laws on the subject at all. And only two states, of all the states that ratified, did integrate their schools after the amendment; but no evidence exists that they did so because of the amendment.

Now we can go on at greater length than I have, or perhaps than you have patience for, into the details of the ratification of the Fourteenth Amendment, but I make this assertion without the slightest doubt that it will stand, when I conclude, not much dented: the framers of the Fourteenth Amendment intended nothing at all about education. And what is more (a point we will get into, I do hope at some length, since we've talked about the principle of *stare decisis*), the Supreme Court of the United States did not, until 1938, think it applied to the subject of education. (There is a hair-raising case, from the point of view of conservatives like Dr. Hutchins, that was decided late in the nineteenth century which, as a matter of fact, allowed the states to go ahead and provide no schools *at all* for Negroes, not just equal schools for Negroes; the Supreme Court recognized the states' utter and plenary control over education.)

Now what happens, ladies and gentlemen, when the Court looks at a document of this kind, our Constitution— knows what it was meant to accomplish—and then says in effect to its constituency out over the country, "Look, we really don't much care what went on in 1868, and really don't much care what Plessy *vs.* Ferguson said, because 'we can't turn the clock back,' [to quote the Warren Court]; we must rather view situations as they exist today"? What does this mean in terms of the decision making process of the United States? I say it means among other things that the major questions of our public policy are consigned no longer to the democratic process, but are consigned precisely to nine men who may or may not (but in *this* case do) act as spokesmen for ideology in the United States. And I wonder whether or not any of us (even people at the Center for the Study of Democratic Institutions) are prepared henceforward to have major policies in the United States decided in that fashion.

There are those who say, "Well, if you don't like what the Supreme Court did, why don't you amend the Constitution?" This is a cute argument, but the point it misses is that before 1954, here we were in the United States in the middle of a vast disagreement about how to handle our racial problem in the field of education, how to handle it on a national basis, and neither the one side nor the other could possibly command a constitutional consensus that would approve a fixed constitutional provision. And consequently, we worked on the problem through what I like to call the "fluid processes" of our Constitution, the organic mechanisms of our society. And then all of a sudden the Supreme Court comes along and says, "Oh, but *our* solution is now *in* the Constitution, and so it is now up to you people who would like to keep your schools segregated to go out and get the hard constitutional consensus of three-fourths of the states and two-thirds of the Congress to get the matter back where it was in the first place."

And then we come, even as I come close to the end of my time, to the argument that, well anyway, the Supreme Court has spoken. And since it has spoken, we all must obey. The Supreme Court's decisions, after all, are "the supreme law of the land." Well, I guess the first answer to that is that, "No, the Supreme Court's decisions are *not* the supreme law of the land." There is nothing in the Constitution of the United States that says any such thing, certainly nothing in the supremacy clause that says any such thing, nor is there any implication to that effect. Now, the judicial supremacists often concede this point but say, "But you've got to take into account that the American

tradition prior to 1789 had recognized the idea of the
judges' prerogatives and consequently the framers could
assume judicial supremacy would be incorporated into
the Constitution without them mentioning it." But no, that
isn't true either. The fact of the matter is that the principle
of judicial review *itself* was not accepted by the American
tradition in 1787, let alone the idea (which I urge you to
understand is a quite different idea) that other branches
of government would be bound by the Court.

"Well, okay," the supremacists say, "let's grant that, but
surely it's true that during the debates at the Constitutional
Convention or in the Federalist papers, all of this came
out. A new doctrine was going to be inaugurated." But no,
that isn't true either. As any historian familiar with the
period knows, neither the debates on the convention nor
the Federalist papers affirm any such thing as judicial
supremacy.

But then we are told, "If that's not true"—and Dr.
Hutchins has alluded to The Great Man—"anyway John
Marshall brought it into our way of doing things. He made
the Supreme Court's decisions the supreme law of the
land." But no, he didn't do that either. What Marshall did
do was to inaugurate the practice of judicial review. But
neither he nor any subsequent Supreme Court—until the
present Court, in the case of Casper *vs.* Aaron, decided in
1958—claimed that when the Court has spoken other
branches of government must follow suit.

And then when that is conceded, the supremacists say,
"Well, all right, but the point is that the country has *acted*
as though the Supreme Court were the final arbiter for all
of these years." But obviously that cannot be true either
because all of us (even those of us who are not historians
but are only reasonably adult and have passably retentive
memories) can think back to 1937 and 1938 when the

Supreme Court decided what it thought was the law of the land, only two or three years later to decide that something else was the law of the land. And what happened in between was that the President and the Congress indicated that they were about to punish the Court for having made a mistake about the Constitution.

So this theory, I am saying, is of rather recent vintage; and before we are through tonight I hope we will have more time than I have right now to explore what the basic understanding of the American consensus has always been.

And roughly let me say it to you now: it is that all of the various power centers in the United States have an obligation under the Constitution to cast their own interpretation on that document. And precisely the genius of the American system has been the preservation of tensions between these branches on the understanding that ultimately they will work out a compromise solution, if you like, but some consensus solution that will be dictated by the community at large. That is the way our government has worked in the past and the way this conservative dearly hopes it will work in the future.

Robert M. Hutchins

Rebuttal:

Mr. Bozell has misunderstood me. I did
not say that I propose to sail under the conservative banner. I said that any conservative should sail under *my*
banner. I do not, for example, understand Mr. Bozell's
position with regard to judicial review. We have had it in
this country ever since the First Judiciary Act, as far as
state legislation is concerned. It was state legislation that
was involved in Brown *vs.* Board of Education. I should
think that it would be quite revolutionary—much more
than liberal, it would be *radical*—to propose now, after
the long history that we have had, in which the Supreme
Court has declared legislation in the states unconstitutional, to hold that they had not such power or could not
exercise it.

Mr. Bozell suggests that I am some kind of romantic
educator in proposing, doubtless from force of habit, that
the Constitution is a charter of learning. But what else can
you make of it? What does one do with Mr. Chief Justice
Marshall talking about "we must never forget that it is a
constitution that we are interpreting?" What is one to do
with the absence of *stare decisis* in constitutional cases, a

topic on which I take it everybody is agreed? It is precisely because nobody in his right mind (to say nothing of the Founding Fathers, who had very good minds indeed) could suppose that the conditions of later years were going to be those of 1787 to 1789; that precisely because of this they could not have done that. They were too intelligent to do that. We *must* regard the Constitution as a charter of learning.

When I say "a charter of learning," I don't mean that it is a blank check to spend our national resources, intellectual or other, in any way; but the Constitution cannot bind to specific forms of action that in the nature of the case were unforeseen at the time the Constitution was adopted. I refer again to Mr. Chief Justice Hughes, who talked of "the seeds the Fathers planted."

In the course of exercising its undoubted power to review the legislation of the states, the Supreme Court has in the past struck down many acts (of many legislatures) of which I heartily approve. I regard the whole tendency known as substantive due process as most unfortunate, thwarting developments in this country that should have been permitted. I go with Mr. Justice Holmes in his dissenting opinion in 1905, in which he said that the Constitution was not intended to enact Mr. Herbert Spencer's *Social Statics.*

But we have this power in the Supreme Court, unless we propose to make now a radical break with our past. The thing to do is what Lincoln said he would do about the Dred Scott Case. Lincoln did not say, "I am going to disobey it, or see to it that it is disobeyed." Lincoln said, "I am going to try to get this decision reversed." And this is certainly the kind of action that I would recommend to anybody who sincerely believed that Brown *vs.* Board of Education was a bad decision.

Mr. Bozell suggests that the Supreme Court has to play by the rules of the game, and if they don't play by the rules of the game they have in some way become constitutionally immoral, or unconstitutionally moral. But my whole point is that this is what they did! They had a constitutional statement, the Fourteenth Amendment, adopted under different conditions—totally different conditions—both with regard to the Negro and with regard to education. They had to decide whether, given the conditions of 1954 and not the conditions of 1868, the seeds that the Fathers of 1868 planted would result in the opinion of 1954. Litigation about whether or not the states had any obligation to supply actually equal—not separate but equal—education to Negroes began with the decision in the Gaines Case in 1938.

You had then a long, continuous debate, and a debate not merely in the Court, but a debate in the country, a dialogue, a political dialogue, a process of learning in the country about what the situation was.

The Court has to interpret the Constitution. Even Mr. Justice Black does not literally mean that the plain words of the Constitution settle anything. These plain words are far too general and too abstract. The Court, then, must interpret these words. What must a Court do? Is Mr. Bozell saying that they can never do anything except what they did before? And that if they said something by way of a dictum in 1896, they have to say it *again* in 1954? Suppose they all recognized that Mr. Justice Harlan, the first Mr. Justice Harlan, was right in dissenting in Plessy *vs*. Ferguson in 1896? Must they still repeat the verdict of the majority? If they are not literally bound, then, to repeat the mistakes of the past, how may they alter those mistakes? Plessy *vs*. Ferguson does not seem to me to be very good sociology or very good law. I do not see any

reason why the Supreme Court, having reached the conclusion that it was neither good law nor good sociology
nor good public policy, should feel bound to adhere to it.

I must say that I really don't understand what Mr.
Bozell is talking about when he says that the Supreme
Court made itself, in this case, spokesman for an ideology.
What in the world is ideological about saying that a Negro
is a human being? What is ideological about saying that
the whole public policy of the United States since the Civil
War had been to make the Negro a first class citizen just
like everybody else? What is ideological about saying that
"the Constitution is color blind"? Mr. Justice Harlan, who
was born in Kentucky, made that statement in 1896. This
result has now been achieved. It has been achieved in
accordance with the constitutional tradition of the United
States.

L. Brent Bozell

Rebuttal:

Brown *vs.* Board of Education didn't say any such thing! It said that southern schools, or schools all over the country, had to be integrated. It didn't say anything at all about Negroes being human beings. It said that a certain kind of *educational* process in the United States was desirable in order for Negroes to achieve their full maturity and not to feel inferior. It said something, in a word, about education. It attempted to provide a national *rule* for education. And as I tried to say earlier, my point is not that this rule is a *wrong* rule, but my point is that the Constitution of the United States does not authorize a national rule about education.

And if you want to know what the "ideology" involved was, it is precisely the ideology that says that this vague notion of equality between human beings should be *so* elevated in our visions and in our programs that *every other consideration* is put aside—even the consideration I regard most vital to the preservation of the American society, namely the observation of our constitutional rules of government.

Dr. Hutchins has insisted that *stare decisis* does not

apply in constitutional cases. Up to a point he is right. Most
of us think it does not. Most of us think that when the
Court looks at a wrong decision it has made on a constitutional case, that it ought to look into it again and see what
decision the Constitution indeed ordains. And I have no
objection at all, or I would have had no objection at all
back in 1954, if the Supreme Court had said, "Look, the
rule that *some* people think was ordained about education
in Plessy *vs.* Ferguson is wrong, and therefore we ought
to find out what the Fourteenth Amendment *really* ordained." I would have had no objection at all to this. The
point is that the Court did *not* do that. If it had done that,
it would have gone back to the amendment and found that
education shouldn't have been the concern of the Court at
all. It would have gone back to its original decisions in the
Cumming and Gong Lum cases, which we may yet talk
about.

Dr. Hutchins says that "Oh, we can't always go along
with the Court when it makes its mistakes." But what
criteria do we use? What criteria have been suggested here
tonight? The nearest one that I have found identified is a
kind of an afflatus, a kind of inspiration that some of us
seem to feel has been bestowed upon us to understand
what is best for the American society. All of us *have* these
kind of inspirations from time to time, but the question is
whether we should inflict them on the rest of the American
people as constitutional law!

Dr. Hutchins said, in a sort of deferential condemnation
of past Supreme Courts, that he didn't believe in the rule
of substantive due process, which the late nineteenth century Court affirmed. Well, I don't either. He said the
reason he doesn't believe in it (and I don't purport to quote
him exactly) is something to the effect that it inhibited
social progress and so on. Well, I think it did that too. But

that isn't why I oppose it. I oppose it because the Fourteenth Amendment did not *authorize* substantive due
process. It did not authorize the Supreme Court to say to
the states, "Look, you can't pass social reform laws."
These laws were within the states' prerogatives under the
Tenth Amendment. And so I am in utter agreement with
him that the Supreme Court not only makes mistakes, but
makes atrocious mistakes sometimes. But where we seem
to disagree is what we should *do* about it.

Well, what the states did in that case was to go right on
passing their social reform laws until the Supreme Court
changed its mind. And the question arises today, What
ought *we* to do about this? What ought the states to do
about their disapproval? And my answer (which I shall be
glad to specify later on if you press me to do it) is that the
touchstone of prudence ought to guide us precisely as it
guides the school children in Massachusetts who go right
on praying, despite Justices Black and Douglas. Without
having federal troops march into the schoolroom, they
go on praying under the full authority of the state of
Massachusetts. If, however, there is a problem of an
incipient riot and great civil disorder, then I would urge
that if a governor of a southern state is not prepared to go
to jail, and so let himself be martyred for this principle,
then what he ought to do is what the authors of the Kentucky and Virginia resolutions did—very esteemed men,
men who had something to do with the writing of the
Constitution—which was to say, "Never mind what the
Congress is doing. Never mind how it and the Supreme
Court is interpreting the Constitution. We have our *own*
interpretation and we will go out and solicit the support
of other states, and of the rest of the American community,
and see if we can't bring about a change in the thing."
And I say this is a far different thing from abjectly agree-

ing to the thunderous pronouncements of *The New York Times,* that once the Supreme Court has spoken we all must behave ourselves like good constitutional citizens.

Dr. Hutchins has professed to be perplexed by what I understand by judicial review, or to what extent I support it. I support it not because it was written into the Constitution, but because it indeed has been ratified by practice. But as I tried to say earlier on, we have simply got to remember the distinction between the Court's right to make a decision in a given case—to cast its own interpretation upon the Constitution with regard to the litigants involved in that case, and then to look out upon the country and say, in effect, "Do I have your support?" It's one thing to say that. And it's another thing to say that once the Supreme Court has spoken, thenceforward Congress, the President, and the states have their hands tied—must regard the Supreme Court decision as part of the Constitution itself.

And if this be regarded as an insolent view, let me suggest that Abraham Lincoln had much the same one. He said during his first inaugural address (and I regard this as a representative statement of the American consensus down to the recent affliction): "The Supreme Court's decisions must be binding in any case upon the parties to a suit as to the object of that suit, while they are also entitled to very high respect and consideration in all parallel cases by all other branches of the government." I would underline this: *may all other branches respect the decision, consider its validity, weigh it.* And Lincoln went on to say, "But at the same time the candid citizen must confess that if the policy of the government, upon vital questions affecting the whole people, is to be irrevocably fixed by decisions of the Supreme Court the instant they are made in an ordinary litigation between parties in personal actions, *then* the people will have ceased to be their own rulers, having to that extent practically resigned their government into the hands of that emminent tribunal."

Lincoln's view, *despised* today by our learned commentators! Lincoln's view, not one formed unaware of the tradition of the Federalist papers and the American Constitution itself and what had gone before it (and, as a matter of fact, not unaware or not unperceptive as to what was going to come in the future).

What I've tried to say is: until the modern judicial supremacists tried to persuade the American people that the Supreme Court's word is something like Stalin's, we were all, most of us, agreed that the Supreme Court was but *one* department of government in this country—a department covered with the obligation to interpret the Constitution according to its own lights with respect to the framers of the Constitution. But only *one* such department. And other departments—the members of which took the same oath of allegiance to support the Constitution as members of the Court did—*also* were obliged to support the Constitution.

You may despise Governor Wallace, but what is Governor Wallace to do when he looks at the document as we have discussed it tonight and sees that his state is free to determine its own educational policy? . . . and here are these federal marshals out in the corridor telling him, "No, that is all wrong. You have got to do something else. If you don't, there's Walter Cronkite and Edward Murrow, and they will say enormously bad things about you." What is Governor Wallace to do—Governor Wallace, whose hand was once upheld as the Constitution required him to uphold it, asserting, "I swear to support the Constitution of the United States"? Can he abdicate that responsibility to

Earl Warren? I think that if he does so, then the hopes all of us have in maintaining a society in which our major decisions are the function of the popular will, rather than the latest intuitions of our social engineers, are forever doomed.

L. Brent Bozell

Conclusion:

W ITH RESPECT TO THE question of the actual nature of the decision in the Brown Case, I think it ought to be said that one would not be far wrong in assuming that a sociological judgment was the basis of the Court's decision. I quite agree with Dr. Hutchins that Gunnar Myrdal didn't play a very large role in that, and I wouldn't much care if he did. But the Court quite *clearly* said that it had concluded (how it concluded it specified in a footnote) that segregated education breeds a feeling of inferiority in the Negro—and if that is not a sociological judgment, I don't know what is. And mind you, I have no objection to having recourse to sociologists about this; they know more about sociology than anybody else. What I have objection to is having recourse to sociology in Supreme Court decisions.

The question before the Court, it seems to me, was what the Constitution *prescribed*; and was not what either a majority or a minority of sociological opinion in the United States regarded as beneficial to the development of children. Ordinarily that kind of consideration is one that is presented in due form to the *political* bodies of the United States, the state legislatures and the national legislature. And if that is not a solution suitable to the majority, the constitutional majority of the people of the United States, what they can do is go and amend the Constitution via Article Five.

I have been accused by Dr. Hutchins of prescribing a rule for anarchy. "How can you possibly disobey a decision," he says. "What you've simply got to do is work to reverse it." Well, is this true in every case? Is there anybody here who cannot think of a decision of the Supreme Court that would be so absurd that he would not think of obeying it, or that he would not think of having his public officials obey it? Suppose the Court should decide tomorrow (and don't mind me if I'm fanciful because this is my point, to be fanciful) to suspend the 1964 presidential election on the grounds that the Constitution says nothing about popular balloting. Are Messrs. Johnson and perhaps Goldwater to start writing their memoirs as a result of this? Should they wait for the Court to change its mind? Or suppose the Court should decide that every state ought to give an annual endowment of $100,000 to the Center for the Study of Democratic Institutions as the part of advancing its program for promoting equal protection of the laws. Should the states hand over their checks, pending a reversal of the Court's opinion? Would Dr. Hutchins accept the checks?

Now these are examples *reductio ad absurdum* to be sure, but if there are exceptions to the rule he suggests, then there is something wrong with the rule. And the easy answer, "Ah, but we must use reason in this case," begs the all-important question: namely, *whose* reason? The Supreme Court's? Well, that takes us right back to where

we started, doesn't it? Well, whose then? Dr. Hutchins'?
Mine? Governor Wallace's? Not any one of these is good
enough for us.

Our traditional way of doing things is to draw on the
combined resources of our various branches of government and the people, and to try to work out a consensus
on the problems that trouble us; and not to entrust final
authority to *any* branch of government.

And I go on thinking that there may be some who feel
that this approach is unfeeling and insensate, that it doesn't
respond altogether to the country's passion of the moment
or even to the better impulses of its conscience. Perhaps
you feel it's time, as we're told, for America to right the
wrongs that it has committed for 150 years, as Presidents
Kennedy and Johnson tell us. (The bumper stickers say,
"Freedom Now." And my own church, in Washington,
has as a matter of fact substituted for the post-Mass
supplications to the Almighty to assist in relieving Communist lands from atheism and tyranny, prayers for justice
and charity to Negroes.)

We are told, and told increasingly, that the American
people have incurred a primary obligation, in this day of
ours; and that is to do penance for their sins against the
Negro race. And all of this is very moving, as long as it is
kept in proportion and we keep other important things in
mind too. And it moves me. But I deplore the abandonment
of the standard of prudence in choosing the relevant means
to reach that end.

I'm reminded of an answer that Garry Wills recently
gave in *National Review* to James Baldwin—Baldwin,
who had maintained in effect, "Down, or I'm through, with
the American way of life! Western Civilization is a farce!
To hell with Christ!" Wills came back and said, in effect,
"Look, Baldwin, the Negro and the Negro race has such

hopes and has such aspirations as it does precisely because it is now a part of Western Civilization. Because of the Christian vision and the Christian way of doing things, the Negroes can hope for political progress and social progress; but this progress will depend upon the maintenance of the social and political institutions that govern Western society."

And my addition to that commentary is that the Negro is well reminded today that the constitutional morality which we have been talking about is something in which he has an enormous stake. Wreck it and you wreck not only America's way of doing things, her hopes for stability and well ordered liberty; you also probably destroy the Negro's last best hope for achieving justice and earning love.

Robert M. Hutchins

Conclusion:

I BELIEVE THAT Mr. Bozell's presentation is
a combination of literalism, cynicism and alarmism. I also
think that there's some confusion of identity here. Mr.
Bozell has been debating, a large part of the time, against
those who believe and practice sociological jurisprudence,
against *The New York Times*, against learned commentators who say that "the decision of the Supreme Court is
forever emblazoned," etc. I am none of those things.

I merely say that the decision of the Supreme Court
on the segregation of the schools is legally and morally
right! Anybody who wants to hold that it is legally and
morally wrong should do what Lincoln did. I don't think
Mr. Bozell should use Lincoln on both sides of an argument. What Lincoln said was that he was not going to
disobey the decision in the Dred Scott Case; he was going
to see if he could get it reversed.

Now, I think this whole thing turns on this literal,
simplistic view of the Constitution that Mr. Bozell has.
Mr. Bozell *believes*, actually believes, that you can look
at the words of the Constitution, no matter when they were
written—1787, 1789, 1868—and that these words will

tell you what to do! Well they won't; they won't. I have asked Mr. Bozell repeatedly to tell us, *since* they won't, what it is he is going to do? Where is he going to get his interpretation? There has to be an interpretation.

Now Mr. Bozell answers with what I regard as cynicism. That is, he portrays these nine eminent gentlemen on the Supreme Court as sort of whimsical lads (or operatives of some pressure group, probably sociological, certainly ideological). But these people are trained lawyers—they went to law school, got admitted to the bar, are accustomed to hearing arguments from the most distinguished lawyers in the world. To think otherwise would be revolutionary indeed.

The Supreme Court of the United States has been appointed in the same way since the Constitution was adopted. There has been the greatest disagreement with its opinions and this disagreement is fine. I'm all for it. But to say that what you have here is a whimsical, lightheaded group of people, is simply an outrage. And Mr. Bozell illustrates this by his fantasies of checks for the Center for the Study of Democratic Institutions. You don't have to think that way. These are people brought up in the tradition of the bar; used to practicing the tradition of the bar. They are aware of the history of the law, and they are aware of the American idea. And it is their responsibility, under the Constitution, to interpret the American idea to us under contemporary conditions and in the light of the Constitution and the amendments thereto.

Sociology: Plessy *vs*. Ferguson is *nothing* but sociology! It is the sociological statement of 1896, of the way the people felt in various parts of the country. The decision is reached on this basis. This is a serious, responsible enterprise in which the Supreme Court is engaged! And simply to assume, because you don't like the *decision*,

that therefore you have here some light-headed fly-by-
nights who are bleeding hearts and probably read Communist literature (or read literature written by the father
of a Communist)—this is absurd!

Now, since you have to interpret the Constitution, what
are you to interpret it in the light of? The answer is that
you are going to interpret it in the light of the responsible
dialogue conducted about the American idea and its realization today—the responsible dialogue about the human
idea of justice and what it means in America today.

I say again, Brown *vs.* Board of Education is a declara-
tion that the Negro is a human being, and is a citizen, and
that his education is therefore of the first importance to
him and to the United States.

Mr. Bozell draws his light from plain words that are
opaque. I draw my light from the illumination of the
American tradition!

James MacGregor Burns

vs.

Willmoore Kendall

The Congress

"Resolved: The deadlock in Washington
is to be deplored."

James McGregor Burns

Opening Statement:

It's a wonderful thing to come across this great country, from Massachusetts to this magnificent area, but I must confess that I came here under some duress. I came here because I believe in the kind of thing that the sponsors of this debate are giving to this community. Yet, I talked to a friend of mine in Massachusetts who's a Californian and I happened to mention that I was coming here. He's a liberal and he looked at me with great doubt and said, "I don't know if you ought to go out to Pasadena. They're all conservatives out there. They won't listen to you. They've already made up their minds." And I argued with him. I said, "Why would they come to a debate if they had?" He was adamant about this. And he left me with the parting crack, "Be sure you get a visa before you go into Pasadena."

I think the fact that I'm here indicates how *I* felt about this little discussion. I'm flattered and delighted to be invited to talk with you and to debate with Mr. Kendall the subject of Congress. I also came because I wanted the opportunity to debate with Mr. Kendall, who is one of the foremost members of our profession of political science, a

distinguished conservative theorist, and a person who has
kept political science as well as the nation's press in something of an intellectual ferment. And that's a very good
thing.

Now I'm not going to make any particular argument
about the existence of a deadlock in Congress. It seems to
me the existence of a deadlock is quite clear—if by deadlock we mean the ability of Congress to frustrate the President's program and the promises made by the two—and
I say two advisedly—political parties in the previous presidential campaign.

The real question that we're concerned about tonight is
whether this deadlock is to be deplored. And we don't
know whether the deadlock is to be deplored unless we
ask, What is being deadlocked? And I think the answer is
quite clear: the civil rights bill, and indeed all the major
proposals made by presidents in the last fifteen years, except for voting, have been deadlocked in Congress. Aid to
education (federal aid to education aside from higher
education) has been deadlocked in Congress. Medicare
has been deadlocked in Congress. The establishment of
wilderness areas to a great extent has been deadlocked.
Cultural exchange programs have been deadlocked. Foreign aid has certainly been drastically reduced. Aid to
urban areas for transportation and similar pressing problems has been deadlocked.

Now that list that I've just given you—and I could give
you a much longer list—is a very personal list. Many of
you probably (if my report on Pasadena is correct) don't
share my sense of urgency about the things that are deadlocked and the things that should be done. And everybody
must make his own personal decision as to whether he is
satisfied or not that these programs have been deadlocked.
I won't debate that particular issue. What I do want to

debate, and argue—where I think there is a great gulf between liberals and conservatives—is how we go about
attacking the problems that I've listed. Because I would
imagine that even though we may be deeply divided here
tonight as to the urgency of governmental action on these
problems, I'm sure that many here agree that these problems do exist. I imagine that many of us here are concerned about the health of the aged, and about the quality
of education, and about fair treatment of Negroes and
other minorities—even though we may have very different
ideas as to how to go about dealing with these problems.

Some conservatives would like to solve such problems
if the job can be done exclusively by private enterprise—
perhaps for profit. Hard experience, it seems to me, indicates that many of these jobs can be undertaken only by a
coalition of government and private enterprise. But at this
point, and certainly at the point where it seems clear that
some of these problems can be undertaken only by government, the typical conservative throws up his hands and, I
think all too often, gives up the effort. And why does he
give up the effort? Because he feels that government not
only will bungle the job, but will deprive people of their
rights and liberties and freedoms in the very process of
bungling it. And that's a pretty tough combination.

And this brings me to what I think is the essence of the
dispute today between American liberals and American
conservatives. It seems to me that the typical conservative
all too often has a blind and unreasoning hostility to government action. On the other hand, it seems to me that the
liberal, as *I* see him, is willing to use government where
as a practical matter government can do the job. And why
does the conservative so often, and sometimes blindly,
oppose government? He does this because he has been
brought up on the notion that "the more government,

automatically the less liberty." "The more government, *automatically* the less individual liberty, the less individual freedom."

This, I contend, is at the heart of our dispute! And this, I contend, is one of those oversimplified notions that may sound good in theory, but is about eighty per cent wrong in practice.

The position of the liberal, at least *my* kind of liberal, is this: government *can* be a vital instrument in extending people's liberties. Now please note the word "can." American liberalism (again, the kind of liberalism that I'm trying to speak for tonight) does not endorse the idea that "the more government, automatically the more individual liberty"—just as we do not endorse the opposite idea. It may be that socialists, and certainly it's true that Communists, usually believe that "the more government the more freedom," if they happen to believe in freedom (which the Communists don't—at least our kind of freedom).

The point I am trying to make about liberals, and the thing that decisively separates the liberals of this nation from socialists (creeping socialists, *any* variety of socialists!) is that *we take a pragmatic, practical view toward the possibilities of using government to expand individual freedom.* We simply assert that government *can* be an instrument to expand freedom—just as private organizations, like businesses and universities and civic organizations, can also be such instruments.

In short, we liberals propose that we approach each situation affecting the enlargement or narrowing of individual freedom, with a simple question, What kind of action (private or public) or what kind of institution (a government agency, a business corporation, a foundation) is best suited to deal with this situation?

Often liberals will want to use *both* public and private methods. For example, liberals believe that the freedom of the American Negro can be expanded *not* through government alone, *not* through private agencies alone, but by both public and private organizations working in partnership along the whole spectrum of equal job opportunity, education, voting, school integration and the like.

Now maybe this is a rather obvious point. Certainly it should be. But conservative spokesmen and publications in this country have clouded and confused popular thinking on this matter through their blind and unreasoning hostility to government. *Of course* they don't mind governmental deadlock in Washington, because they do not see the enormous potential of government for good—that is, the potential for expanding individual freedom.

Let me dwell on this basic point just a minute further. Hobhouse once said that freedom is a matter not simply of the increase or decrease of restraints, but of the reorganization of restraints. His point is that we're all under restraints, from all sorts of sources. My students at Williams College are under restraints from deans and professors and family and the campus police and so on, just as they have many ways of expanding their freedom through private activities, through their college, and, I would say, through government.

There's a profound truth in Hobhouse's remark that the problem we face is the reorganization of restraints. Any time government acts, it may well limit the liberty of some people to some extent. If the government taxes me more, it cuts down the variety of things that I can buy, and that's a limitation on my freedom.

The question is, to what extent is the government enlarging someone *else's* freedom, or perhaps even enlarging *my* freedom *in another area?* If the government, for example, takes money from me and uses it to build or help build a vocational school, which in turn trains an unemployed man in a new skill, which that man uses to get a good job, which in turn pays him well and hence tremendously enlarges his freedom, *then* the government is increasing the net total of all our individual liberties.

Or the government may take my money (indeed does take my money, and all too much of it sometimes it seems to me) and use it for national defense. This will narrow my freedom again to use my earnings as I would like, but obviously it immensely broadens my freedom in that a strong national defense protects *all* our liberties.

The only way clearly to tackle this question is to talk in terms of specifics. And I'll be happy to talk specifics all night. In fact I *insist* on specifics, because only with specifics can we get away from what seems to me this wrong conservative idea that "the more government, automatically the less liberty."

Now just to apply this point to one crucial area, it seems to me that the most important specific today is civil rights —especially the freedom, the individual liberty, the individual opportunity of the Negro. And we're going to have to do a lot of computing, a lot of adding and subtracting, to think intelligently about civil rights.

Take the famous case of "Mrs. Murphy." Mrs. Murphy runs a small boarding house and may wish to exclude Negroes. This is her idea of freedom. (And I respect her desire for freedom.) But there is also the case of the traveling Negro family—hot, tired, looking for a place to stay. Mrs. Murphy's boarding house is a public accomodation. She is offering her place to the public for private profit. So we simply have to balance two conflicting concepts of freedom here.

Now anyone who *really* believes that her right to exclude

overbalances the right of that family to get a room and a meal at a public accomodation, that it overbalances the right of that family to avoid what might be bitter psychological effects of being turned away from the door and of driving another five or fifty miles for a place to stay—that person has a right to be against the civil rights bill.

But *most* Americans, I believe, have a different way of balancing those two claims. And these are the liberals in the broadest and best sense of the word—people who believe that that door (Mrs. Murphy's door and the doors of many other public accomodations) should be opened wide and that in the long run this is the best thing, not only for the person who walks through that door, but also for the person who threw the door wide (even though the door was thrown wide in response to a law and not, unhappily, in response to an impulse of generosity in Mrs. Murphy herself).

I hope very much that Mr. Kendall will address himself to this problem tonight; first of all because he's about the best person in America to take the conservative approach to this kind of question, and secondly because it seems to me, as a reader of the *National Review* and many other conservative publications, that this is indeed the crucial question separating liberals and conservatives in America.

Now just one final point, before I finish, because it is also very much a part of this dialogue: I've often discovered, in talking with fear-minded conservatives who are concerned about these problems, that if you talk with one long enough he may finally rather glumly admit that maybe government has to play some role in dealing with some of these problems. But then he often retreats to a second line of defense. He says, "Okay, maybe government has to do it, for various reasons; but it must be local government. And if it's not local government it must be

state government. But try to keep the federal government
out." Well, I'm going to perhaps upset you a little more
tonight and contend that that question too should be ap-
proached in a very practical frame of mind.

This idea, that (automatically or by definition) "If you
have to have government, it should be local government
rather than the national government" is, I think, part of
the conventional wisdom of our time. It is an idea that
rests on no final evidence. I would say that the answer to
this question depends again on the practical situation:
what kind of problem has to be tackled? And there are
many local problems that should be tackled by local government. But in a nation that has become increasingly
centralized, urbanized, where the independence of the
local community has been breaking down because of the
basic social and economic trends in the country, it just
happens that the federal government (and this has been
shown time and time again) has to move in with the tremendous strength, the tremendous resources that it has.

For example, to take the famous case of the condition
of the Tennessee valley in 1932: a lot of people might
have hoped or preferred that the local governments deal
with that local problem, or the regional government if
there had been one, or the state governments. But the
problem was that those governments were the governments
least capable of dealing with the condition of the Tennessee valley. And it took the national government, in a very
controversial thing called the TVA, to mobilize the
strength of the nation and to make TVA (which may not
be wholly appreciated by some Americans) literally a
showcase for millions of people from other parts of the
world.

But I don't want to base my point on any one example
because my point is that, *It depends on the situation. I*

think only one generalization is permissible in this area, which is: often the very states and localities that most need help are those least able to provide it.

Ultimately, it seems to me (if I might end again on a rather theoretical note) that this question of the level of government ought to be put in a kind of moral framework. One reason I think I'm a good American is that I believe in America as a nation—not just as something to salute or to talk about or to sing to. To me the greatness of the nation is that we do pool its resources. The greatness of this nation is that I *can* help a Negro in the South or a white in the North, if I happen to make a larger income than he does. It's *fine* with me, if through the instrumentality of our federal government there is some effort to equalize the conditions of this man with my own.

In short, this is the way we pool not only our strength in this nation; it's a way we pool our compassion. And it's because I feel that in the long run—with all its inefficiencies (and we political scientists are well aware of the inefficiencies of government), with all the things that we worry about in government, with all the human failings in government—our government (national government as well as state and local government) is the *best* instrument because it is the most democratic instrument. It is the popular, responsive instrument for working together, for pooling our strength, for drawing together the great potential, both of the economy and of the hearts and minds and talents of Americans. Because government has *that* kind of potential, and because we do have, in my mind, these problems that I listed at the beginning—for these reasons I believe that the deadlock in Washington today is truly to be deplored.

Willmoore Kendall

Opening Statement:

I CONFESS that Mr. Burns leaves me worried about whether we're to have a debate here. I've listened with fascination as he attempts to state the issues between liberals and conservatives (as he understands them), but with all the more fascination because I happen to be an avid fan of Mr. Burns and his writing. And I've heard him say very little that I would have expected him to say. Let me, at the risk of spoiling this occasion for everyone, say that I, at least, am not the kind of conservative who moves from the axiom, "the more government the less freedom." Neither am I the kind of conservative that has a net preference for local and state action rather than federal government action. I'm equally willing with Mr. Burns to let these questions be decided on their merits. What concerns me, and what I would have expected Mr. Burns to be concerned about (though I well know the difficulty of setting forth so complex a position as his in a mere twenty-five minutes), is how we are *going to make decisions* here in America about the kind of problem that lies so heavily upon Mr. Burns's heart.

112

In my opening remarks, therefore, I am going to try to come to Mr. Burns's assistance and get us a debate—by drawing not merely upon the speech he has just made, but upon my vast knowledge of his writings. And I will try to get a quarrel going between what I regard as the Burns position as set forth in his books, and the Kendall position as set forth in mine. (Mostly—let me say at this point—I concede Mr. Burns's major points in his opening remarks.)

Mr. Burns has, as we see him here and in his books, two complaints: first, that Washington is a place where nothing happens; second, that nothing happens when nothing happens in Washington. To put it a little differently: first, there is "deadlock" in Washington, and second, that deadlock is more than flesh—well, more than Mr. Burns's flesh—can bear. Something ought to be done— *must* be done as Mr. Burns argues in book after book—to end the deadlock and to prevent similar deadlocks in the future.

Let us dispose, initially, of his first complaint—that there is "deadlock" in Washington. Now on the *factual* side, let me say at once that I have very little quarrel with Mr. Burns here. Congress does indeed—month after month, session after session, decade after decade—refuse in general to pass the legislative proposals rained upon it from the White House. Mr. Burns wants to call that state of affairs "deadlock," and the congressional stance that produces it "obstructionism." And I say, Let us be generous with Mr. Burns and try to bring out into the open, and understand, why this curious use of language com-

mends itself to him; and, happily, we do not have to go
very far afield in order to find parallels that will help us
to understand.

Take, for instance, the thief who attempts repeatedly to
burgle a certain house, and cannot do so because the
double bolt on the door foils his best burgling techniques.
From the thief's point of view, from the thief's family's
point of view, even from the point of view (which brings
us back to Mr. Burns) of the thief's mouthpiece, the owner
of the house (who put the double bolt on the door) is
indeed an obstructionist. And the state of affairs between
the thief and the owner of the house (all those well-laid
plans, all gone aft-a-gley!) is indeed deadlock. More, we
should be guilty of lack of *empathy* if we did not understand why they (the thief, the thief's family, the thief's
mouthpiece—Mr. Burns) latch onto words like "deadlock" and "obstructionism." We can understand the curious use of language, yet I hope still keep on using language
correctly ourselves and still keep ourselves reminded of
how to put it in English, namely: from the standpoint of
law and order, from the standpoint of justice, the owner
of the house is a citizen rightfully defending his property—
not an "obstructionist." The state of affairs between him
and the thief is the successful prevention of burglary, not
"deadlock"; and the thief is—well, a thief.

Or again: from the standpoint of, say the anti-social
monster who would like to see the towns in the valley
inundated, who would like to see the population of the
valley drowned—from the standpoint of any such anti-
social monster, I say, the dam that holds back the waters
is obstructionist and the state of affairs between the dam
and the waters is that of deadlock. We will waste our time
arguing with him about his use of words. Our task is,
rather, to recognize (despite the verbal mist he surrounds

himself with) that he and ourselves are looking at one and the same state of affairs: the dam does indeed hold back the waters, mercifully sparing the towns and people of the valley; we simply put it differently: what he calls deadlock we call the successful protection of the valley against floods; what he calls obstructionism we call the civilized control of potentially dangerous natural forces; where he deplores, we reverently say, Thank God! And no, my point is *not* that "it all depends on the point of view"; I will not, I trust, be suspected of any such relativism. Precisely not: my point is that there is a *right* use of words and a *wrong* use of words; that the way the thief and the anti-social monster in the valley use words is (though understandable) *wrong*. And our use of words, as I have just illustrated it, is *right*.

So, too, with the way my distinguished opponent uses words. He and his friends (to paraphrase a hero of his) think not of what they can do *for* America, but only of what they can do *to* America. He and his friends have (for the purpose of doing things *to* America) a *program* (the thing Mr. Burns seems most concerned to talk about here) which they are *determined* to carry out (so determined, as some of Mr. Burns's friends like to say these days, that they "will not take no for an answer"). They are determined to carry it out because, firstly, being the sort of people they are, and given the sort of thing over which their hearts go pit-a-pat, they *like* that kind of program. So much is understandable. But there is a second reason, which is: they believe, or say they believe, their program would contribute to the happiness and well-being of the American people (which is perhaps less understandable).

Now because of a queer quirk in the process by which we elect our presidents, Mr. Burns and his friends—let's begin now to call them by their right name, which is "the

liberals"—normally dominate the White House (or, if you
like, are always able to put a liberal in the White House,
who goes into the White House with their program already
in his pocket. The liberal just leaving the White House
has another copy in his pocket as he goes out the door—
just in case he'll be coming back some day.) The new
President sends their program, bit by bit, bill by bill, over
to one of his flunkies in Congress, who, one by one, drops
the bills into the hopper. Congress then proceeds—the one
with one bill, the other with another bill—either to sit on
the bills until adjournment or, if the President is able to
force a showdown, to vote them down, or if not vote them
down then pass them in such emasculated form that the
liberals protest (quite properly) that they are not *their*
bills, their program, at all. Congress, of course, sits on the
bills, or votes the bills down, or emasculates the bills, because it is opposed to anyone's *doing* to America what the
bills propose to do; because it believes the bills would accomplish *not* the happiness and well-being of the American people but the misery and degradation of the American people; because, in a word, the program, bill by bill,
is an assault on the congressmen's most strongly held con-
victions, an affront to their deepest loyalties and beliefs, an
outrage to their conception of the destiny of America.
Congress hurls the bills back into the teeth of the President
and the liberals in the same manner, and in much the same
mood, in which a self-respecting nation would hurl back
the advance columns of an invading army.

Mr. Burns wants to call that "deadlock." The majority
of Congress, naturally enough, want to call it protecting
the country against the extremist proposals of the liberal
intellectuals. Mr. Burns wants to call Congress "obstructionist." We, the people, who biennium after biennium
elect a Congress that *will do just what Mr. Burns says*

Congress does, think of it as defending our way of life against those who would undermine and destroy it. Mr. Burns and his friends want to call the Congress that strikes the President's program down a "do-nothing" Congress. We, the people, who elect and re-elect such a Congress— elect and re-elect such a Congress with what Mr. Burns must deem *monotonous* reiteration—think that such a Congress, far from doing nothing, does a very great deal: it does *just* what we send it to Washington to do.

Yet (as I have intimated all along) we must not quarrel with Mr. Burns merely about words: he is saying nothing that cannot be translated out of the tortured jargon of liberalese into plain English. What he means is that Congress won't do what he and his friends *want* Congress to do and (despite his strange use of language) we can, I repeat, understand him—nay, must understand him, because he is "a problem" (a problem, moreover, that we the people who elect the Congress must learn, somehow, to deal with). And we may count ourselves fortunate to have Mr. Burns for a whole evening under our microscope, where we can hope to find out what makes him tick.

What more can we say to Mr. Burns—what more is conceivably *worth* saying to Mr. Burns—about his complaint that nothing happens in Washington, that there is a deadlock? At least, I think, this (though in order to say it we are going to have, this time, to ask him to do the translating, because I do not know how to say it in liberalese): Mr. Burns likes to talk about deadlock, about obstructionism in Washington, because, I submit, he does not want to face political reality—political reality as it is given to us in contemporary America. Mr. Burns likes to talk about deadlock and obstructionism because that implies that the *trouble* is in Washington—that is, in the nation's political *machinery,* about which Mr. Burns usually writes—in the nation's political institutions and practices, where it may lend itself to solution along the kind of lines that have always fascinated minds like Mr. Burns's (along lines, that is to say, of political *gadgetry*).

Give Mr. Burns and his friends a free hand with our political machinery (and I hope he will tell us a little more about his plans in that connection), let them do a little tinkering with it, and everything (so Mr. Burns and his friends like to think) will come out all right! All of which is to say, Mr. Burns and his friends will then get their way in American politics: the White House program will be adopted, and all good things will be added unto us. And I do think it worth saying to Mr. Burns, You mistake your problem. You are treating a surface manifestation of your problem for the problem itself. *We* understand why you are hurting, but you yourself do not understand what is hurting you. The deadlock, if you still insist on calling it that, is not in Washington, but out in the country; and yes, I repeat, I do think that is worth spelling out for Mr. Burns here on the very threshold of our debate.

What is political reality in contemporary America? Mr. Burns says, Political reality in America is our faulty *political* machinery [and again I urge him to come to that central theme of his in his reply], which keeps my friends and me from getting our program adopted. I say, Political reality in America is that we Americans disagree profoundly on the *merits* of that program. Mr. Burns says, Ah! But the program is *good;* it alone will enable America to live up to the imperatives of the age [I cite Chapter one of his recent book] to fulfill its historic destiny. And I say, But exactly what we Americans disagree about, on the deepest level, is what the imperatives of the age are and what *is* the historic destiny of America. But, Mr. Burns will reply (a little disingenuously, perhaps), How could people possibly disagree about things like *that?* Is it not *obvious* that we must carry out the civil rights program? That we must wage and win the war against poverty? That we must broaden and deepen social security? That we must learn to coexist peacefully with World Communism? That we must get the federal government busy solving our transportation and urbanization problems? And so on down the line? And I answer, patiently, No, no, Mr. Burns, *none* of that is obvious; the things you mention are, if I may put it so, the bones of contention. But, Mr. Burns asks (for at last I have captured his attention!), How can *that* be? And I answer, Well, look; what it amounts to is: some of us here in America are liberals, whose hearts do go pit-a-pat over the program you sketch. And some of us are conservatives, who dislike the program very much. Then Mr. Burns, who at least in his writings tends to avoid those words "liberal" and "conservative" that we suddenly find him using tonight, asks (a little incredulously perhaps), What's *that* got to do with it? And I answer, Well Mr. Burns, to begin with, just this: some of us think there are vastly *more* conservatives in America than there are liberals, and that political reality in America (what you call "deadlock") merely reflects a failure on the part of the liberals to plead their case successfully before the tribunal of public opinion.

It is here, let us pause to note, that the automatic response we can expect from Mr. Burns becomes most interesting: We have *not* failed to plead our case successfully, he will say. We have all the best arguments on our side—as witness our strength in the nation's academic community, among the nation's top columnists and television and radio commentators, on the editorial pages of the nation's leading newspapers; on foreign policy, we have on our side the great experts on international relations and Communism; on fiscal and tax policy and on welfare legislation we have with us the great names in economics; on civil rights, we have with us the bulk of the nation's clergy and the great names in constitutional law (including of course the learned justices of the Supreme Court); on reapportionment, on enfranchisement of the southern Negroes, on Congress, we have with us *en masse* the nation's political scientists. How can you say that we have not pled our case successfully before the tribunal of public opinion? And I answer, Not good enough, Mr. Burns; all you prove is that the liberals plead their case successfully *with one another!;* that you find each other *infinitely* persuasive (which I never doubted for a moment).

My point is that you have failed to persuade—I take the phrase from a great political philosopher—the "generality of men amongst us"; that you have failed to create a consensus in favor of your program; that, so far as we know, the liberals are still a small minority in the American community; that—to come back—the deadlock you *should* be worried about occurs out in the cities and towns and villages and farms of America, out among the American people themselves. And that deadlock has got to be stated in terms something like this: the militant minoritarian liberalism for which you speak has run up against a blank wall of conservative opposition; it is *not* just Congress that rejects your program, it is *we the people* as articulated through the Constitution that *we* ordain and establish. It is *we* who reject your program; and you, Mr. Burns, you and your friends, are clearly powerless— powerless at least under the existing rules—to do anything about it! Political reality in America is that the liberals don't have the votes. More, the liberals, finding themselves called on at last to explain why liberal solutions don't work, are fresh out of ways to enlist new voters. The liberal program, to put the matter in its simplest terms, lacks sex appeal. And let any reader of this debate who doubts that go to what learned folk like Mr. Burns and myself call the *locus classicus*—namely, the pages of Mr. Burns's recent book, in which he tells of his own unsuccessful race for Congress. Mr. Burns appears to have persuaded everyone in his constituency except . . . well, the generality of the voters. He does not need *me* to explain to him the political reality the liberals are up against. In order to get the picture he has only to go call on his neighbors.

But let us pass on to Mr. Burns's second complaint: nothing happens when nothing happens in Washington. Mr. Burns deplores the fact that nothing happens in Washington—the fact, that is, that Congress consistently bids the President (if I may put it so) to go roll his hoop. And Mr. Burns thinks that when nothing happens in Washington, something ought to happen about it, something ought to be done about it (a question, I say, to which he returns in book after book). He has strongly-held and carefully-worked-out ideas as to what ought to be done; and it is of the first importance that we should grasp the real bearing of what he has said repeatedly he wants us to do about it.

Since he and his friends *cannot* win under the existing rules, he asks us to *change* the rules so that he and his friends *can* win. Indeed, if we were to translate his basic proposal into the language of, say, basketball, it would run something like this: Our team loses all the time, and clearly has no prospects of winning in the future. But that is because the existing rules confer overwhelming advantages on our opponents; and I'm here, I, Mr. Burns, am here, to tell you where exactly in the existing rules the bias occurs. The trouble, clearly, is this whole business of having the baskets at the two ends of the court the same size. Let us forthwith double the size of the basket at one end of the court, and make the basket at the other end of the court exactly the size of the basketball. And let it always be understood that we liberals play toward the end of the court that has the larger basket. Things'd be different from *then* on!

Things would indeed be different from then on. I agree completely with Mr. Burns (though without taking back what I have said earlier) that the adoption of certain gadgets would improve the prospects of the liberal program and the prospects therefore of breaking the deadlock in Washington. Redraw the lines that demarcate our congressional districts, so as to give city folk more representatives—and the liberals will, no doubt, pick up a few Congressional seats. Abolish the seniority principle in congressional committees, abolish the filibuster—and you will, no doubt, weaken the hold we conservatives have on the easiest method for frustrating the President. Go still further, if you like, and eliminate somehow those troublesome mid-term elections that Mr. Burns and his friends worry so much about—and again, things will look up for the liberals. Though not to an extent that I for one would lose any sleep over. The baskets at the two ends of the court, as far as I'm concerned, would still be the same size, and the conservatives would still win the big games. But that is because I have not yet mentioned what we may call Mr. Burns's Special Gadget (as set forth in his latest book).

Nobody, I venture, knows better than Mr. Burns that the modest changes in the rules that I've mentioned up to now—the modest changes proposed by Mr. Burns's predecessors in the attack on the American political system—

won't turn the trick. Won't, that is to say, dish the conservatives. But Mr. Burns has left his predecessors so far behind
in this regard that when he looks back over his shoulder
he can't even see them. *They* proposed, as *the* means of
cutting the Gordian knot, what they called the responsible
party system: let our two parties become, respectively, a
Conservative Party and a Liberal Party; let them, at
election time, offer the American people a genuine choice
between competing sets of policies; let the people, in their
quadrennial elections, themselves decide the destiny of
America; let us end the White House-Congress stalemate
by putting both President and Congress under one and the
same freely-arrived-at popular mandate. Mr. Burns, I repeat, is not to be confused with those earlier, Casper
Milquetoast would-be reformers of the American political
system. Mr. Burns, fed as he is on the red beef of Machiavellism, proposes nothing less than a *coup d'état*—and,
along with it, an ingenious scheme for bringing it off:

Let the liberals—he calls them the Presidential Democrats and the Presidential Republicans, but we have no
difficulty identifying them—conspire together to capture
both parties. Let us have, instead of a Liberal Party and a
Conservative Party, *two* liberal parties (each of which will
offer the electorate only liberal candidates). Let us, in
effect, remake all our elections in the image of our presidential elections, so that no matter how a man votes, he will
vote (or at least seem to vote) for the liberal program. That
is Mr. Burns's proposal for ending the anti-liberal bias of
the existing rules; and I have, by way of conclusion, three
small things to say about it.

First, the very shape of his proposal concedes my main
point here this evening: the liberals have failed to plead
their case successfully before the tribunal of public
opinion.

Second, the proposal, on the face of it, justifies the claim I have made in the language of basketball: what Mr. Burns *really* deplores is the baskets being the same size for both his team and his opponents.

Third, the proposal runs hard up against what I like to call the Dilemma of the Little Gingerbread Boy. The Little Gingerbread Boy, you remember, couldn't run 'til he got hot, and couldn't get hot until he ran. And Mr. Burns's proposal—which stripped of irrelevancies is a proposal for eliminating from our system what he calls the one-party congressional constituency, the congressional constituency constantly dominated by a single one of our political parties—is up against that same difficulty. Before you can eliminate the one-party congressional district, you must eliminate the one-party congressional district, and you can't do *that* because of the one-party congressional district.

In short, there are no short-cuts that will get Mr. Burns and his friends their program. Like it or not, they are going to have to do it the hard way—by persuading the American people (the American people moreover acting not by mere majority vote but by consensus) to adopt the program as their own. I do not—I hasten to add—exclude the possibility that the liberals may, in the long run, accomplish that miracle of persuasion. But in the long run, as Lord Keynes is there to remind us, we are all dead.

James MacGregor Burns

Rebuttal:

I THINK Mr. Kendall has given a very significant talk tonight. I think indeed that his talk could be considered—and may be considered in the long run—an historic milestone in the development of conservative thought in the United States. Whether you think this is a good milestone is something that those who are conservatives will have to decide for themselves. I have rather mixed feelings, because I believe in a continuing debate between liberals and conservatives. I would really hate to see the day when only one of these two sides dominated the country indefinitely. And yet, I fear that Mr. Kendall has so sacrificed and so watered down the conservative cause of this nation as to leave it in some disarray by the end of his opening statement. And because of that (as I say, I do believe in the continuation of this dialogue), I'm deeply troubled.

First of all he made, it seems to me, a tremendous concession when he said that conservatives, or at least his type of conservative, would be willing to consider governmental action on its merits. If he really believes this—and if his belief here is shared by most American conservatives—it means that an historic shift *is* taking place in American conservatism from the old type of conservatism that we associate, perhaps wrongly, with men like Mc-Kinley or indeed Democrats like Cleveland (that is, the idea that that government is best which is the least government, or the least government is the best government), and from the idea of *laissez-faire* (the idea that we ought to keep government small; the Coolidge idea that the business of America is business, not government). This, it seems to me, is an historic transition, from that nineteenth and early twentieth century concept of American conservatism to the modern British-type conservatism exemplified by men like Winston Churchill and Harold Macmillan, who, as you know, believe in social welfare programs far in advance of those put forward by American liberals and by the Democratic Party in the United States.

Whether it is good for conservatism to make this transition . . . again, is for you to say. But I hope no one here will miss the significance of what Mr. Kendall has conceded tonight. And it's because he is the kind of honest and insightful man that he is, that he's willing—facing the facts of our national life— to *make* this concession that makes him a much more interesting conservative spokesman than the conservative who stands up and blindly opposes government action. All I can say though, is this: if he is making this concession, if we are witnessing this milestone, it seems to me that he ought to communicate this to the journals for which he writes, because I think any fair reading of those journals will suggest that they still do support that nineteenth century concept of conservatism that I just described.

But the main point of Mr. Kendall's remarks is, I think,

a more serious concession to liberalism. And one again (perhaps rather perversely) that deeply troubles me. To me the striking thing about Mr. Kendall's presentation tonight, in all its eloquence, is that he finally was willing to play what many conservatives call "the numbers game." He finally is willing to base his concept of what is good for this nation on a question of public opinion, on a question of numbers, on a question of who has the most votes.

Now I happen to believe in that kind of decision because as a liberal I believe in majority rule and majority rule is a question of adding up "bodies" (or, I hope, adding up minds). I believe that the great decisions *should* be made by numbers, by forty-nine million as against forty-seven million (or even, unhappily, with smaller differences than that), because I believe that majority rule is ultimately the way a democracy must be run and the only way it can effectively be run.

I should be saying this, and I will defend this; but the fact that Mr. Kendall again and again would turn to concepts like "we the people," and to concepts like public opinion, and to concepts like the vote, and how many people vote and what they're voting on, in presidential elections as against off-year elections—this too represents what I feel to be a dangerous concession, on the part of conservatism, to liberalism. I wish he had spent more time defending conservatism as such. I wish he had spent more time defending the great conservative tradition—whether it's a Burkean tradition or a *laissez-faire* tradition, that would be for him to say. But what worries me (and what indeed seems to me from a debating standpoint to be too great a concession) is his playing this numbers game. Because as soon as the conservatives start to base their principles on numbers, *then* they're playing the liberal game (what they call the liberal game; what I would call sub-ordinating their basic values to a liberal premise, which is the premise of majority rule).

Now this came out particularly in his discussion of the Presidential Party and the Congressional Party. It came out particularly in his discussion of presidential elections as against off-year elections. And, to a great extent by implication, it came out in his discussion of extending the right to vote.

I will be prepared to argue at long length (and, I think, with many impressive statistics) as to how the American people feel about this deadlocked program. And I would produce as evidence the results of the last forty years of presidential elections and the results of most of the congressional elections of those forty years. I would produce those elections in which there have been clear confrontations between liberal and conservative leaders—between Republicans who were really conservatives and Democrats who were really liberals. And what interests me is that, in presidential election after election it has been the candidate offering the liberal program who has won the election. And I would not exclude Dwight Eisenhower in '52 and '56—and I don't think that most conservatives would exclude Dwight Eisenhower in '52 and '56—because Dwight Eisenhower won those campaigns partly as a result of the great place he occupies in American public opinion based on his contributions, but largely because he was willing—and if you doubt this please look at the Republican Party platforms of those two years and look at what Mr. Eisenhower promised in those two years—to make liberal promises (and to give him credit, once in office he made a great effort to live up to many of those liberal promises).

In short, if you can accept the presidential election—

with its two parties and their platforms, with its two candidates laying out their programs before the people day after day in the fall—as a fair test of how the American people feel, as an honest presentation to them of the issues that divide the country, then it seems to me that the historic result is most emphatic: the American people for the last forty years, *have* been voting for liberalism, *have* been voting to unpadlock (to use the term that Mr. Kendall likes so much) the American Congress.

Mr. Kendall was good enough to refer to my own case of running for Congress. I made a deliberate decision in 1958—and I think it's a decision that conservatives would respect as well as liberals—that I would run on a platform that I really believed in and not one that was simply tailored to what I thought might be the majority wish of the district. Yes, I got my answer. I was defeated. I concluded, as a liberal must conclude, that fifty-five per cent of the voters in my congressional district preferred the platform of my Republican opponent to mine. I'm willing to accept that decision. I've never debated it or pleaded against it. But it seems to me, by the same token, that if we're to interpret the results in that First Congressional District of Massachusetts as a conservative decision, then we should interpret the presidential decisions of the last forty years as liberal decisions. And these are the *national* decisions; these are the decisions in which *all* the American people take part.

And indeed, if we're going to play this numbers game that Mr. Kendall has *forced* me to play tonight (and of course again I'm happy to have the excuse to play it), *compare* the total number of votes in the presidential elections and the congressional elections. *Note* the number of congressional districts in which ten or twenty per cent of the people vote. *Note* the number of congressional districts in which a fair set of alternatives was not presented to the voters in that district. And compare that again with these two presidential campaigns that were televised and carried by the press and ask yourselves again: If you're going to make the decisions by numbers as liberals want and not in terms of intrinsic merit (as I thought that conservatives wanted), then it seems to me that the issue is quite clear: rightly or wrongly, in the long perspective (and I'm enough of an historian to admit that the final decision will lie in the future), we happen to be in a liberal era in this nation. I think the day will come when we'll be in a conservative era. And I think it's good that a nation has a breathing spell. I think it's good that we have the pendulum moving back and forth. But that time may not yet be with us; this will be a judgment of the American people. And as long as we go by majority decisions (as Mr. Kendall evidently wants us to do), then we're going to have to do what the majority wants.

And so, I would hope that we will *not* conduct this debate completely on the basis that Mr. Kendall wants to conduct it. I hope that before the evening is over, Mr. Kendall *will* bring us back to the historic bases of conservatism as he sees them, and will restore in all their importance, in all their relevance, the great conservative traditions that inform the life of this nation.

Willmoore Kendall

Rebuttal:

N OW WE'RE getting somewhere!

But two quick points. First, let Mr. Burns not try to confuse the issue into which I am attempting to draw him, by pointing to the literary weeklies and fortnightlies and monthlies that profess to speak for American conservatives. Mr. Burns very well knows from my book that *my* conservatives are the voting majority of the Congress which is not today and has never been properly confused with those end-of-the-nineteenth-century Supreme Court justices who talked all manner of natural law foolishness and thus attempted to frustrate the Congress of the United States.

Second, let Mr. Burns not confuse things by pretending to summon me back to the historical bases of conservatism in America. The historical bases of conservatism in America have to do with the American political system, and not with the content of the decisions that that political system produces. As I understand it—as Madison and Hamilton understood it—the sky has always been the limit about the content of those decisions, provided the proponents of the several decisions won their victory within the rules of

131

the system as they were orginally laid down in the Constitution and in the Federalist papers. Mr. Burns is just as
interesting to me as I to him. He is the liberal of liberals
because it is he who challenges us conservatives *on our
political system itself*. It is he who says that it is a bad
political system; he who has the most ingenious plan for
remaking it.

Having said that let me get really down to business. In
my opening remarks I spoke of Mr. Burns as constituting
for the rest of us "a problem" that we must learn somehow
to deal with, and we have now got him on record in his
rebuttal as the kind of "problem" I see him as being. I also
took the liberty, you will remember, of referring to his
Machiavellism. And now that we have the second speech
of his tingling in our ears, I perhaps owe it to you—if only
in the hope of driving our discussion to the deepest level
of disagreement between Mr. Burns and me—to say why
I deem him a problem and what I mean when I describe
him as a Machiavellian. Mr. Burns is a problem, because
—let me lay it on the line—of his blind devotion to (and
I might add his peculiar understanding of) what we political scientists call the majority principle—and I am now
speaking to Mr. Burns directly on his accusation about
"the numbers game."

Think back over what he has said explicitly; think back
even more carefully over what he has tacitly assumed,
tacitly taken for granted, and you will see that I do him
no injustice when I speak of his blind devotion to the
principle of majority rule. And he's now about to try to
convince you that I also am blindly devoted to it.

Mr. Burns, I submit, is absolutely committed to the
following proposition about how we should govern ourselves here in America: in a democracy, he confidently
believes, the majority has a *right* to call the turns about

policy. Democracy, that is to say, *is* majority rule—his very words of a few moments ago. In a democracy, the outvoted minority has therefore (we must understand) a duty to accept and to obey the policy directives of the majority. *The* problem in a democracy is (as it has always been for Mr. Burns in his books) to *get* yourself your majority and then get on with whatever jobs you have mobilized your majority for. (Mr. Burns's picture of Jefferson in his last book is highly relevant in this connection.)

Whether the outvoted minority is going to *like* your policy directives, whether the outvoted minority *can* accept those policy directives and continue to find political life tolerable, whether or not the outvoted minority will in fact *obey* your policy directives—these are questions that a man like Mr. Burns feels no need to discuss or even raise with himself. The majority principle, the right of the majority to have its way, the duty of the minority to obey (for example, the duty of the white Southerners to obey the policy directives of the civil rights program, if and when it is enacted)—these things figure in Mr. Burns's political philosophy and in that of his friends as, quite simply, Higher Dogma, as self-evident truth that requires no demonstration or justification, as the This Is It Boys of American democracy.

If that is not what Mr. Burns believes, I call upon him to tell us in the course of this debate what it is he believes that is recognizably different from that. While, if it *is* what he believes, I call upon this audience to agree with me that Mr. Burns is indeed "a problem." For Mr. Burns's Higher Dogma is, I contend, novel doctrine in our democracy—so novel, I contend, that most of us cannot hear it stated, cannot hear it put into words, without shuddering.

Mr. Burns's understanding of majority rule is not, I

contend, the American understanding of majority rule.
The American understanding of majority rule is: yes, the
majority decides; the numbers are taken, they are counted;
in a sense the numbers do prevail, in a sense it is a numbers game. Concretely however, the majority of our *elected
representatives* decide, *not* the majority of the electorate
—but decide, in any case, subject to two clearly understood provisos:

First, the majority decides precisely with an eye to
whether or not the minority *will* obey, can be counted
upon to obey—with an eye, therefore, to the necessity of
carrying the minority with it. And second, that we Americans are for some purposes, but only some, a nation
capable of making decisions by majority rule, and for other
purposes not a nation (Mr. Burns will recognize that I am
merely reading him the basic doctrine of the tradition of
the Federalist papers)—not a nation—but a federation of
states in which majority rule has no status and no meaning. We have no tradition here in America for the kind of
majority rule that is prepared to say to the minority (as
Mr. Burns would not, I think, hesitate to say to the white
Southerners on civil rights, or on the seniority principle),
You are going to obey our policy directives *because* we
are the majority. You are going to obey because if you do
not obey, we are going to *make* you obey.

We have, I repeat, no tradition in America for that kind
of majority rule. And anyone who *talks* that kind of majority rule in America becomes by that very fact "a
problem." Why? Because that kind of majority rule won't
go down in America. Because the preconditions for that
kind of majority rule are not present in America. And
because the man who talks that kind of majority rule in
America is consciously or unconsciously preparing the
inevitable breakdown of the American political system.

The American political system is not and never has been a system for the automatic acceptance of majority mandates by the minority. It is not and never has been a system for the large-scale coercion of the minority (which is what at *every* point Mr. Burns's program is going to require). Under the American political system *the majority bides its time until it can act by`consensus* (which is ultimately the *opposite* of the numbers game)—that is, in conditions where it can reasonably expect the minority to go along. And I say, There is grave question whether the American political system can digest a Mr. Burns, who is simply not interested in consensus.

So too with my point about Mr. Burns's Machiavellism —for, let me hasten to say, I use the term Machiavellism in its strict technical meaning among political scientists (without, of course, any implication that Mr. Burns is particularly wicked or particularly unscrupulous, by comparison with the rest; only more ingenious than most of us). My point is quite simply that Mr. Burns, like Machiavelli, *is in full rebellion against the whole political tradition to which he was born.* Mr. Burns, like Machiavelli, refuses to subordinate himself to the norms of political discourse as his fellow citizens understand it. Mr. Burns, like Machiavelli, stands forth before his fellow citizens not merely with novel proposals, but also with a new kind of political thought—a new kind of political thought that they, his fellow citizens, can only find *shocking* once they begin to understand it. For Mr. Burns's quarrel with the American political system is in the last analysis, first (and again I refer to his books), that it is not a good system for translating the will of the majority (which he equates with the will of the people) into action. And second, that it is not a good system for getting the government to do things for the people.

Now, at the risk of sort of pulling the rug out from under Mr. Burns in this debate, I am going to concede *both points*. It is *not* a good system for translating popular will into action. It is *not* a good system for getting government to do things for the people. If what we want in America is a system for translating popular will into action, and for getting things done for the people, then the system ought indeed to be reformed along the lines Mr. Burns proposes.

But, as Mr. Burns well knows off at the back of his mind, the system was *never* intended for translating popular will into action, or for getting government to do things for the people. And if Mr. Burns is sincere in summoning me back to the tradition, he would have to expect me to adopt just the position that I am adopting. Our system was devised by men who feared and disliked *above all things* the operation in politics of sheer, naked will (men therefore who were not given to using language like "the will of the people"). It was devised for purposes that had nothing to do with simplistic formulae like "the will of the people" or "government doing things for the people." It was devised to bring about amongst us a more perfect union, thus not to divide us into majority and minority. To assure us the blessings of liberty, thus not to keep us busy coercing one another. Above all: to achieve the ends of justice, thus not to effectuate the will of any group amongst us, but rather to reconcile the conflicting claims of *different* wills amongst us. It was devised to effectuate not the will of the people, but rather, as *The Federalist* puts it, the deliberate sense of the community, the *whole* community, as to what ought to be done, what policies ought to be adopted.

Most of us, I believe, still think that these are the right purposes for our political system to have. And we still think, therefore, that it is the best political system we could possibly have. That is why, after fifty years of attacking the system for its alleged anti-majoritarian bias, Mr. Burns and his friends have got, well, exactly nowhere as regards the acceptance by the American people of their proposals—which begin with J. Allen Smith and flow directly in a straight line right to Mr. Burns. That is why we Americans will look askance at anyone (even so persuasive an advocate as Mr. Burns) who seeks to give our system a Machiavellian twist in the direction of the sheer naked will of the majority.

Willmoore Kendall

Conclusion:

BEFORE BEGINNING my summary, I'd like to pose two quick questions to Mr. Burns—in the hope that he will touch upon them in his own final summary. I would like to ask him, as a political theorist, about his characteristic doctrine—the notion that any American majority is ipso facto a moderate majority. I follow that in connection with the Eisenhower majority. I follow it in connection with the Goldwater majority. I do not see how it could possibly be true of any future *liberal* majority, since it seems to me that within the spectrum of American public opinion, the liberal proposals are precisely *extremist proposals*—extremist proposals on the face of them—which explains the general character of the sort of quarrel they kick up amongst us.

The second question I'd like to ask is, I would like a little more clarification of his peculiar distinction between things the majority has a right to do and things that it doesn't. First, I would like to know the source of the distinction (or whether it is merely an arbitrary distinction Mr. Burns imposes upon the majority principle). Secondly, how does he explain that civil rights turns up, so to speak, on both sides of the equation? With one side of his mouth Mr. Burns tells us [in the question period—Ed.] that the majority must not touch civil rights and that he hopes that the Supreme Court will police them if they try to. With the other side of his mouth he is clearly hoping for a majority action for the civil rights bills. So he is hardly excluding civil rights from the general sphere of the majority, and he leaves me quite confused.

As for my summary, it, happily, can be very brief. Ever since I first learned of this debate, I have sort of looked forward to it as a peculiar debate. In an ordinary debate, one supposes, the two principals at least go through the motions of trying to persuade each other, trying to transform each other into converts. (Or failing that, at least each principal tries to pick up a convert or two out in the audience.) Not so tonight. Mr. Burns and I—engaged as we are in exactly the same racket—have been eying each other across a chasm for lo these many years. Neither of us, I suppose, thought to coax the other over to his side of the chasm here, or even much expected that the chasm would be particularly narrowed in the course of our exchange.

What we did hope, I like to think, was that we would get our respective positions out on the table where both ourselves and the audience could look at them more clearly than we've been able to in the past—with each party coming perhaps to *understand* each other a little better (not only the other party's position, but also understand its own position a little better). What I did hope, too, was that we would see to it that both positions in the course of the debate got sharply delineated, so that the audience could see clearly what choices a man is actually making when he takes sides on the issues that divide conservatives and liberals.

That hope, I believe, has been abundantly realized in the course of the evening. The issues do seem to me to be out on the table (particularly those about the future of the American political system) where we can understand *why they are issues* and where, better still, we can see that they are *indeed* issues—that is, questions on which there are indeed two sides, and where each side is capable at least of a certain amount of reasoned argument in its favor.

I'm willing to content myself in this final summary with merely listing the big questions as they seem to me to have emerged in the course of the debate—with the hope that the audience will go away prepared to pursue them further *as issues,* to seek new evidence bearing upon them, to discuss them further so that one day we can hope to see them decided by a genuine American consensus.

Here then are the issues as I understand them here at the end of the evening:

First, do the liberals, as they often pretend, have a majority out in the country? Or am I right in saying that they remain a mere minority? Put otherwise, have the liberals, as I allege, failed to plead their case successfully before the tribunal of American public opinion? Second, are the current liberal proposals for the reform of the American political system (especially Mr. Burns's proposals) dictated by desperation—by a desperate desire to change the rules obviously in favor of the liberals, by a determination to stack the cards in favor of a future liberal victory? Are such proposals, as I contend, liberal attempts to sidestep the responsibility of building a genuine consensus behind the liberal program? Third, does Mr. Burns, as I allege, have a new and dangerous conception of majority rule? And would that conception, because it cannot carry with it the outvoted minority, lead inevitably to a breakdown of the American political system as I have suggested—that is, to the disappearance from amongst us of our most treasured possession, which is government by discussion? Fourth, are we ready, we Americans, to abandon the Federalist dream of governing ourselves by consensus, of governing ourselves by way of arriving (through deliberation, not mere matching of strength at the polls) at a "deliberate sense" of the whole community? Are we prepared, we Americans, to shift the basis of our political system over to reliance on the sheer, naked will of the majority?

Those, then, are the questions I'd like the audience to think further about in the months and years ahead. And if Mr. Burns and myself have helped draw the issues more sharply—helped perhaps to illuminate them a little—I for one shall remember the evening as, well, a happy occasion.

James MacGregor Burns
Conclusion:

FIRST, I WOULD LIKE to express my apprecia-
tion again for this opportunity to take part in the kind of
notable occasion that Mr. Kendall hopes we've had. I
think that Mr. Kendall has set out a good list of differences
between us. I would like to use my brief moments here to
sharpen one or two of these issues.

One of the issues *is* the issue of consensus. The conservative of Mr. Kendall's stripe wants us to wait for more of a
consensus of the people before we embark on economic
and social policy changes. And this is a good traditional
doctrine. Lots of decisions we make in our clubs and private organizations are consensus decisions. But also lots
of them are majority decisions. And again, I would suggest
that it is often a rather common sense question as to when
one has to go by majority rule (and there are those times
that they're rather difficult). But I doubt that anyone can
think of any organization where the majority with which
he has been working has been so ruthless in its decision
that he's felt that it disrupted the whole purpose of the
organization. In short, we live both by consensus and by
majority rule.

Why do I propose majority rule in the area of economic and social change, but not majority rule in the area of civil liberties and the Bill of Rights? I want those bills of rights in the nation and the states always to be there, always supported by a consensus. I never want them changed by a majority. They *do* represent a consensus. But, on this issue of whether we should wait for a consensus on economic and social change, it seems to me that the way we react to that question is simply in terms of whether we want the change.

I don't blame anyone here who's heavily taxed to be upset about how much money—and hence individual liberty, individual choice—is taken away from him by the federal government and used for other purposes. But perhaps I'm just a little bit more sensitive (*perhaps* just a bit more sensitive) to the problem of those whom we're trying to help, especially in terms of their freedom and individual liberty. And it just so happens that millions of Negroes in this country are saying, That consensus of Mr. Kendall doesn't seem to be working. We waited for that consensus to work decade after decade, but it hasn't worked. And the reason they support majority rule is quite simple. As I said at the beginning, your attitude toward the system of government must be influenced—always will be influenced—by the kind of programs you want. And your job as citizens and as thinkers, it seems to me, is to relate your ends and your means. Because these people are tired of waiting for that consensus to come, that never seems to come; they want the government to move ahead under majority action. And let us note that there are those in the civil rights struggle who aren't willing even to settle for that! They want to use direct action. They want to use minority shock tactics.

That's why I believe in majority rule, at least one of the

major reasons I do. It really is a compromise position, between those like Mr. Kendall who will wait decades upon decades for action to take place, and those minoritarians who want to bring about action through direct struggle in the streets. Majority rule *is* a moderate system. But if we're going to keep it as a moderate system, we've got to make it work and we've got to believe in it.

I think this general point may have answered the two or three specific questions that Mr. Kendall raised. He asked me whether a liberal majority was extremist. I don't think it's extremist in either way, because as I said earlier, to get a majority of the nation a party and a politician must broaden his appeal so widely as to make it a moderate point of view.

What does the majority have the right to do? Mr. Kendall asked me. It has the right to do anything in the economic and social arena that is relevant to our national problems and our national purposes—except to change the basic rules of the game. The majority *does* have a right —and this is one of the crucial questions that has come out of this debate—to change *those rules of the game that are not part of our original tradition*. The Rules Committee is not part of the Federalist papers. The seniority rule is not in the Constitution. The filibuster is not in the Constitution or the Federalist papers. These deadlocking techniques are not part of our original system. Indeed, the Founding Fathers expected that the Congress would be the activist part of our national government, to the extent it had an activist part.

It is honestly because I want the conservatives of this nation (when their day comes, when they have persuaded a majority of the nation in a presidential election to their point of view—and perhaps this will be 1964) to have a right to rule in their day—when they have a majority behind them—that I want the liberals of the nations to have a right to rule in what I think is their day today. It's because, as I've said in my book (which Mr. Kendall has been kind enough to refer to quite often tonight), I believe that both liberal and conservative purposes can be realized in this nation, that I hope that we can unlock the great instrument that is a possession of all the people— which happens to be the national government of the United States.

The Combatants:

STEVE ALLEN is one of the most versatile public figures in America. Only 42, he is established as a television performer, author of more than 2000 songs and nine books, Broadway and movie actor, and essayist on subjects humorous and serious. Currently a principal of the National Committee for a Sane Nuclear Policy, Mr. Allen appears here as a defender of the liberal foreign policy.

WILLIAM F. BUCKLEY JR. began his public career in 1951 with a book which rocked the academic community, charging that academic freedom as practiced by liberals was indoctrinating students with an anti-capitalist and anti-religious bias. He soon followed with the founding of the magazine *National Review,* now the nation's largest journal of opinion. The author of five books and lecturing nearly 200 times a year, he is one of conservatism's leading spokesmen.

ROBERT M. HUTCHINS has had a spectacular career as an educator and author. Dean of the Yale Law School at 28, he became president two years later of the University of Chicago. Named head of the Fund for the Republic in 1954, he has since served in that capacity. The author of eleven books dealing with education and political subjects, he is one of America's best liberal thinkers.

L. BRENT BOZELL was graduated from Yale Law School in 1953. Since then he has co-authored *McCarthy and His Enemies,* been an editor of *National Review* magazine and has become, in the words of Barry Goldwater, "one of the most articulate spokesmen for the conservative position

147